MW00623909

THE BEST OF
FANNIE
FARMER

DESSERTS

THE
ORIGINAL
1896
COOKBOOK

This commemorative edition published in 2018 by Publications International, Ltd. is based on the original Fannie Merritt Farmer book published in 1896.

Photographs © 2018 Publications International, Ltd.

Louis Weber, CEO
Publications International, Ltd.
8140 Lehigh Ave
Morton Grove, IL 60053

Permission is never granted for commercial purposes.

ISBN: 978-1-64030-284-6

Manufactured in China.

8 7 6 5 4 3 2 1

TABLE OF CONTENTS.

4 TABLE OF CONTENTS.

CHAPTER III.

CHAPTER IV.

COLD DESSERTS 53

CHAPTER V.

ICES, ICE CREAMS, AND OTHER FROZEN DESSERTS . . 74

CHAPTER VI.

CHAPTER VII.

CHAPTER VIII.

CHAPTER IX.

CHAPTER XI.

CHAPTER XII.

CHAPTER XIII.

12 TABLE OF CONTENTS.

TABLE OF CONTENTS. 13

PAGE PAGE

CHAPTER I.

BEVERAGES.

A BEVERAGE is any drink. Water is the beverage provided for man by Nature. Water is an essential to life. All beverages contain a large percentage of water, therefore their uses should be considered: —

I. To quench thirst.
II. To introduce water into the circulatory system.
III. To regulate body temperature.
IV. To assist in carrying off waste.
V. To nourish.
VI. To stimulate the nervous system and various organs.
VII. For medicinal purposes.

Freshly boiled water should be used for making hot beverages; freshly drawn water for making cold beverages.

TEA.

Tea is used by more than one-half the human race; and, although the United States is not a tea-drinking country, one and one-half pounds are consumed per capita per annum.

All tea is grown from one species of shrub, *Thea*, the leaves of which constitute the tea of commerce. Climate, elevation, soil, cultivation, and care in picking and curing all go to make up the differences. First-quality tea is made from young, whole leaves. Two kinds of tea are considered: —

Black tea, made from leaves which have been allowed to ferment before curing.

Green tea, made from unfermented leaves artificially colored.

The best black tea comes from India and Ceylon. Some familiar brands are Oolong, Formosa, English Breakfast, Orange Pekoe, and Flowery Pekoe. The last two named, often employed at the " five o'clock tea," command high prices; they are made from the youngest leaves. Orange Pekoe is scented with orange leaves. The best green tea comes from Japan. Some familiar brands are Hyson, Japan, and Gunpowder.

From analysis, it has been found that tea is rich in proteid, but taken as an infusion acts as a stimulant rather than as a nutrient. The nutriment is gained from sugar and milk served with it. The stimulating property of tea is due to the alkaloid, *theine*, together with an essential oil; it contains an astringent, tannin. Black tea contains less theine, essential oil, and tannin, than green tea. The tannic acid, developed from the tannin by infusion, injures the coating of the stomach.

Although tea is not a substitute for food, it appears so for a considerable period of time, as its stimulating effect is immediate. It is certain that less food is required where much tea is taken, for by its use there is less wear of the tissues, consequently less need of repair. When taken to excess, it so acts on the nervous system as to produce sleeplessness and insomnia, and finally makes a complete wreck of its victim. Taken in moderation, it acts as a mild stimulant, and ingests a considerable amount of water into the system; it heats the body in winter, and cools the body in summer.

Freshly boiled water should be used for making tea. Boiled, because below the boiling-point the stimulating property, theine, would not be extracted. Freshly boiled, because long cooking renders it flat and insipid to taste on account of escape of its atmospheric gases. Tea should always be infused, never boiled. Long steeping destroys the delicate flavor by developing a larger amount of tannic acid.

How to make Tea.

3 teaspoons tea.   2 cups boiling water.

Scald an earthen or china teapot.

Put in tea, and pour on boiling water. Let stand on back of range or in a warm place five minutes. Strain and serve immediately, with or without sugar and milk. Avoid second steeping of leaves with addition of a few fresh ones. If this is done, so large an amount of tannin is extracted that various ills are apt to follow.

Five o'Clock Tea.

When tea is made in dining or drawing room, a " Five o'Clock Teakettle " (Samovar), and tea-ball or teapot are used.

Russian Tea.

Follow recipe for making tea. Russian tea may be served hot or cold, but always without milk. A thin slice of lemon, from which seeds have been removed, or a few drops of lemon-juice, is allowed for each cup. Sugar is added according to taste. In Russia a preserved strawberry to each cup is considered an improvement. We imitate our Russian friends by garnishing with a candied cherry.

Iced Tea.

4 teaspoons tea.   2 cups boiling water.

Follow recipe for making tea. Strain into glasses one-third full of cracked ice. Sweeten to taste. The flavor is much finer by chilling the infusion quickly.

COFFEE.

The coffee-tree is native to Abyssinia, but is now grown in all tropical countries. It belongs to the genus *Coffea*, of which there are about twenty-two species. The seeds of berries of coffee-trees constitute the coffee of commerce. Each berry contains two seeds, with exception of maleberry, which is a single round seed. In their natural state they are almost tasteless; therefore color, shape, and size determine value. Formerly, coffee was cured by exposure to the sun; but on account of warm climate and sudden rainfalls, coffee was often injured. By the new method coffee is washed, and then dried by steam heat.

In coffee plantations, trees are planted in parallel rows, from six to eight feet apart, and are pruned so as never to exceed six feet in height. Banana-trees are often grown in coffee plantations, advantage being taken of their outspreading leaves, which protect coffee-trees from direct rays of the sun. Brazil produces about two-thirds the coffee used. Central America, Java, and Arabia are also coffee centres.

Tea comes to us ready for use; coffee needs roasting. In process of roasting the seeds increase in size, but lose fifteen per cent. in weight. Roasting is necessary to develop the delightful aroma and flavor. Java coffee is considered finest. Mocha commands a higher price, owing to certain acidity and sparkle, which alone is not desirable; but when combined with Java, in proportion of two parts Java to one part Mocha, the coffee best suited to average taste is made. Some people prefer Maleberry Java; so especial care is taken to have male berries separated, that they may be sold for higher price. Old Government Java has deservedly gained a good reputation, as it is carefully inspected, and its sale controlled by Dutch government. Strange as it may seem to the consumer, all coffee sold as Java does not come from the island of Java. Any coffee, wherever grown, having same characteristics and flavor, is sold as Java. The same is true of other kinds of coffee.

The stimulating property of coffee is due to the alkaloid *caffeine*, together with an essential oil. Like tea, it contains an astringent. Coffee is more stimulating than tea, although, weight for weight, tea contains about twice as much *theine* as coffee contains *caffeine*. The smaller proportion of tea used, accounts for the difference. A cup of coffee with breakfast, and a cup of tea with supper, serve as a mild stimulant for an adult, and form a valuable food adjunct, but should never be found in the dietary of a child or dyspeptic. Coffee taken in moderation quickens action of the heart, acts directly upon the nervous system, and assists gastric digestion. Fatigue of body and mind are much lessened by moderate use of coffee; severe exposure to cold can be better endured by the coffee drinker. In times of war, coffee has proved more valuable than alcoholic stimulants to keep up the enduring power of soldiers. Coffee acts as an antidote for opium and alcoholic poisoning. Tea and coffee are much more readily absorbed when taken on an empty stomach; therefore this should be avoided except when used for medicinal purposes. Coffee must be taken in moderation; its excessive use means palpitation of the heart, tremor, insomnia, and nervous prostration.

Coffee is often adulterated with chiccory, beans, peas, and various cereals, which are colored, roasted, and ground. By many, a small amount of chiccory is considered an improvement, owing to the bitter principle and volatile oil which it contains. Chiccory is void of caffeine. The addition of chiccory may be detected by adding cold water to supposed coffee; if chiccory is present, the liquid will be quickly discolored, and chiccory will sink; pure coffee will float.

Buying of Coffee. Coffee should be bought for family use in small quantities, freshly roasted and ground; or, if one has a coffee-mill, it may be ground at home as needed. After being ground, unless kept air tight, it quickly deteriorates. If not bought in air-tight cans, with tight-fitting cover, or glass jar, it should be emptied into canister as soon as brought from grocer's.

Coffee may be served as filtered coffee, infusion of coffee, or decoction of coffee. Commonly speaking, boiled coffee is preferred, and is more economical for the consumer. Coffee is ground fine, coarse, and medium; and the grinding depends on the way in which it is to be made. For filtered coffee have it finely ground; for boiled, coarse or medium.

Filtered Coffee.

(*French or Percolated.*)

1 cup coffee (finely ground). 6 cups boiling water.

Various kinds of coffee-pots are on the market for making filtered coffee. They all contain a strainer to hold coffee without allowing grounds to mix with infusion. Some have additional vessel to hold boiling water, upon which coffee-pot may rest.

Place coffee in strainer, strainer in coffee-pot, and pot on the range. Add gradually boiling water, and allow it to filter. Cover between additions of water. If desired stronger, re-filter. Serve at once with cut sugar and cream.

Put sugar and cream in cup before hot coffee. There will be perceptible difference if cream is added last. If cream is not obtainable, scalded milk may be substituted, or part milk and part cream may be used, if a diluted cup of coffee is desired.

Boiled Coffee.

1 cup coffee.	1 cup cold water.
1 egg.	6 cups boiling water.

Scald a *granite-ware* coffee-pot. Wash egg, break, and beat slightly. Dilute with one-half the cold water, add crushed shell, and mix with coffee. Turn into coffee-pot, pour on boiling water, and stir thoroughly. Place on front of range, and boil three minutes. If not boiled, coffee is cloudy; if boiled too long, too much tannic acid is developed. The spout of pot should be covered or stuffed with soft paper to prevent escape of fragrant aroma. Stir and pour some in a cup to be sure that spout is free from grounds. Return to coffee-pot and repeat. Add remaining cold water, which perfects clearing. Cold water being heavier than hot water sinks to the bottom, carrying grounds with it. Place on back of range for ten minutes, where coffee will not boil. Serve at once. If any is left over, drain from grounds, and reserve for making of jelly or other dessert.

Egg shells may be saved and used for clearing coffee. Three egg shells are sufficient to effect clearing where one cup of ground coffee is used. The shell performs no office in clearing except for the albumen which clings to it. Burnett's Crystal Coffee Settler, or salt fish skin, washed, dried, and cut in inch pieces, is used for same purpose.

Coffee made with an egg has a rich flavor which egg alone can give. Where strict economy is necessary, if great care is taken, egg may be omitted. Coffee so made should be served from range, as much motion causes it to become roiled.

Tin is an undesirable material for a coffee-pot, as tannic acid acts on such metal and is apt to form a poisonous compound.

When coffee and scalded milk are served in equal proportions, it is called *Café au lait*. Coffee served with whipped cream is called *Vienna Coffee*.

To Make a Small Pot of Coffee. Mix one cup ground coffee with one egg slightly beaten and crushed shell. To one-third of this amount add one-third cup cold water. Turn into a scalded coffee-pot, add one pint boiling water, and boil three minutes. Let stand on back of range ten minutes; serve. Keep remaining coffee and egg closely covered, in a cool place, to use two successive mornings.

To Make Coffee for One. Allow two tablespoons ground coffee to one cup cold water. Add coffee to cold water, cover closely, and let stand over night. In the morning bring to boiling point. If carefully poured, a clear cup of coffee may be served.

After-Dinner Coffee.

(*Black Coffee, or Café Noir.*)

For after-dinner coffee use twice the quantity of coffee, or half the amount of liquid, given in previous recipes. Filtered coffee is often preferred where milk or cream is not used, as is always the case with black coffee. Serve in after-dinner coffee cups, with or without cut sugar.

After-dinner coffee retards gastric digestion; but where the stomach has been overtaxed by a hearty meal, it may prove beneficial, so great are its stimulating effects.

KOLA.

The preparations on the market made from the kola nut have much the same effect upon the system as coffee and chocolate, inasmuch as they contain caffeine and theobromine; they are also valuable for their diastase and a milk-digesting ferment.

COCOA AND CHOCOLATE.

The cacao tree (*Theobroma cacao*) is native to Mexico. Although successfully cultivated between the twentieth parallels of latitude, its industry is chiefly confined to Mexico, South America, and the West Indies. Cocoa and chocolate are both prepared from seeds of the cocoa bean. The bean pod is from seven to ten inches long, and three to four and one-half inches in diameter. Each pod contains from twenty to forty seeds, imbedded in mucilaginous material. Cocoa beans are dried previous to importation. Like coffee, they need roasting to develop flavor. After roasting, outer covering of bean is removed; this covering makes what is known as *cocoa shells*, which have little nutritive value. The beans are broken and sold as *cocoa nibs*.

The various preparations of cocoa on the market are made from ground cocoa nibs, from which, by means of hydraulic pressure, a large amount of fat is expressed, leaving a solid cake. This in turn is pulverized and mixed with sugar, and frequently a small amount of corn-starch or arrowroot. To some preparations cinnamon or vanilla is added. Broma contains both arrowroot and cinnamon.

Chocolate is made from cocoa nibs, but contains a much larger proportion of fat than cocoa preparations. Bitter, sweet, or flavored chocolate is always sold in cakes.

The fat obtained from cocoa bean is *cocoa butter*, which gives to cocoa its principal nutrient.

Cocoa and chocolate differ from tea and coffee inasmuch as they contain nutriment as well as stimulant. *Theobromine*, the active principle, is almost identical with theine and caffeine in its composition and effects.

Many people who abstain from the use of tea and coffee find cocoa indispensable. Not only is it valuable for its own nutriment, but for the large amount of milk added to it. Cocoa may well be placed in the dietary of a child after his third year, while chocolate should be avoided as a beverage, but may be given as a confection. Invalids and those of weak digestion can take cocoa where chocolate would prove too rich.

Cocoa shells.

1 cup cocoa shells.   6 cups boiling water.

Boil shells and water three hours; as water boils away it will be necessary to add more. Strain and serve with milk and sugar. By adding one-third cup cocoa nibs, a much more satisfactory drink is obtained.

Cracked Cocoa.

½ cup cracked cocoa.   3 pints boiling water.

Boil cracked cocoa and water two hours. Strain, and serve with milk and sugar. If cocoa is pounded in a mortar and soaked over night in three pints water, it will require but one hour's boiling.

Breakfast Cocoa.

1½ tablespoons prepared cocoa.   2 cups boiling water.
2 tablespoons sugar.   2 cups milk.
Few grains salt.

Scald milk. Mix cocoa, sugar, and salt, dilute with one-half cup boiling water to make smooth paste, add remaining water and boil one minute; turn into scalded milk and beat two minutes, using Dover egg-beater.

Reception Cocoa.

3 tablespoons cocoa.   A few grains salt.
⅓ cup sugar.   4 cups milk.
¾ cup boiling water.

Scald milk. Mix cocoa, sugar, and salt, adding enough boiling water to make a smooth paste; add remaining water and boil one minute; pour into scalded milk. Beat two minutes, using Dover egg-beater, when froth will form, preventing scum, which is so unsightly; this is known as *milling*.

Brandy Cocoa.

2 tablespoons cocoa.   1½ cups boiling water.
⅓ cup sugar.   4 cups milk.
3 teaspoons cooking brandy.

Prepare as Reception Cocoa, and add brandy just before milling.

Chocolate.

1½ squares Baker's chocolate.   Few grains salt.
4 tablespoons sugar.   1 cup boiling water.
3 cups milk.

Scald milk. Melt chocolate in small saucepan placed over hot water, add sugar, salt, and gradually boiling water; when smooth, place on range and boil one minute; add to scalded milk, mill, and serve in chocolate cups with whipped cream. One and one-half ounces vanilla chocolate may be substituted for Baker's chocolate; being sweetened, less sugar is required.

FRUIT DRINKS.

Lemonade.

1 cup sugar.   ⅓ cup lemon juice.
1 pint water.

Make syrup by boiling sugar and water twelve minutes; add fruit juice, cool, and dilute with ice water to suit individual tastes. Lemon syrup may be bottled and kept on hand to use as needed.

Pineapple Lemonade.

1 pint water.   1 quart ice water.
1 cup sugar.   1 can grated pineapple.
Juice 3 lemons.

Make syrup by boiling water and sugar ten minutes; add pineapple and lemon juice, cool, strain, and add ice water.

Orangeade.

Make syrup as for Lemonade. Sweeten orange juice with syrup, and dilute by pouring over crushed ice.

Mint Julep.

1 quart water.   1 cup orange juice.
2 cups sugar.   Juice 8 lemons.
1 pint claret wine.   1½ cups boiling water.
1 cup strawberry juice. 12 sprigs fresh mint.

Make syrup by boiling quart of water and sugar twenty minutes. Separate mint in pieces, add to the boiling water, cover, and let stand in warm place five minutes, strain, and add to syrup; add fruit juices, and cool. Pour into punch-bowl, add claret, and chill with a large piece of ice; dilute with water. Garnish with fresh mint leaves and whole strawberries.

Claret Punch.

1 quart cold water.
½ cup raisins.
2 cups sugar.
2 inch piece stick cinnamon.

Few shavings lemon rind.
1⅓ cups orange juice.
⅓ cup lemon juice.
1 pint claret wine.

Put raisins in cold water, bring slowly to boiling point, and boil twenty minutes; strain, add sugar, cinnamon, lemon rind, and boil five minutes. Add fruit juice, cool, strain, pour in claret, and dilute with ice water.

Fruit Punch I.

1 quart cold water.
2 cups sugar.

½ cup lemon juice.
2 cups chopped pineapple.
1 cup orange juice.

Boil water, sugar, and pineapple twenty minutes; add fruit juice, cool, strain, and dilute with ice water.

Fruit Punch II.

1 cup water.
2 cups sugar.
1 cup tea infusion.
1 quart Apollinaris.

2 cups strawberry syrup.
Juice 5 lemons.
Juice 5 oranges.
1 can grated pineapple.
1 cup Maraschino cherries.

Make syrup by boiling water and sugar ten minutes; add tea, strawberry syrup, lemon juice, orange juice, and pineapple; let stand thirty minutes, strain, and add ice water to make one and one-half gallons of liquid. Add cherries and Apollinaris. Serve in punch-bowl, with large piece of ice. This quantity will serve fifty.

Ginger Punch.

1 quart cold water.
1 cup sugar.

½ lb. Canton ginger.
½ cup orange juice.
½ cup lemon juice.

Chop ginger, add to water and sugar, boil fifteen minutes; add fruit juice, cool, strain, and dilute with crushed ice.

Unfermented Grape Juice.

10 lbs. grapes.   1 cup water.
3 lbs. sugar.

Put grapes and water in granite stew-pan. Heat until stones and pulp separate; then strain through jelly-bag, add sugar, heat to boiling-point, and bottle. This will make one gallon. When served, it should be diluted one-half with water.

CHAPTER II.

BISCUITS, BREAKFAST CAKES, AND SHORTCAKES.

Batters, Sponges, and Doughs.

BATTER is a mixture of flour and some liquid (usually combined with other ingredients, as sugar, salt, eggs, etc.), of consistency to pour easily, or to drop from a spoon.

Batters are termed thin or thick, according to their consistency.

Sponge is a batter to which yeast is added.

Dough differs from batter inasmuch as it is stiff enough to be handled.

Baking Powder Biscuit I.

2 cups flour.	1 tablespoon lard.
4 teaspoons baking powder.	¾ cup milk and water
1 teaspoon salt.	in equal parts.

1 tablespoon butter.

Mix dry ingredients, and sift twice.

Work in butter and lard with tips of fingers; add gradually the liquid, mixing with knife to a soft dough. It is impossible to determine the exact amount of liquid, owing to differences in flour. Toss on a floured board, pat, and roll lightly to one-half inch in thickness. Shape with a biscuit-cutter. Place on buttered pan, and bake in hot oven twelve to fifteen minutes. If baked in too slow an oven, the gas will escape before it has done its work.

Baking Powder Biscuit II.

2 cups flour.   2 tablespoons butter.
4 teaspoons baking powder.   ¾ cup milk.
          ½ teaspoon salt.

Mix and bake as Baking Powder Biscuit I.

Emergency Biscuit.

Use recipe for Baking Powder Biscuit I. or II., with
the addition of more milk, that mixture may be dropped
from spoon without spreading.   Drop by spoonfuls on a
buttered pan, one-half inch apart.   Brush over with milk,
and bake in hot oven eight minutes.

Fruit Rolls (Pin Wheel Biscuit).

2 cups flour.   ⅔ cup milk.
4 teaspoons baking powder.   ⅓ cup stoned raisins
½ teaspoon salt.   (finely chopped).
2 tablespoons sugar.   2 tablespoons citron
2 tablespoons butter.   (finely chopped).
          ⅓ teaspoon cinnamon.

Mix as Baking Powder Biscuit II.   Roll to one-
fourth inch thickness, brush over with melted butter, and
sprinkle with fruit, sugar, and cinnamon.   Roll like a
jelly roll; cut off pieces three-fourths inch in thickness.
Place on buttered tin, and bake in hot oven fifteen minutes.   Currants may be used in place of raisins and
citron.

One Egg Muffins I.

3½ cups flour.   1¾ cups milk.
5 teaspoons baking powder.   3 tablespoons melted butter.
1 teaspoon salt.   1 egg.
          3 tablespoons sugar.

Mix and sift dry ingredients; add gradually milk, egg
well beaten, and melted butter.   Bake in buttered gem
pans twenty-five minutes.   If iron pans are used they

must be previously heated. This recipe makes thirty muffins. Use half the proportions given and a small egg, if half the number is required.

One Egg Muffins II.

2½ cups flour.	2 tablespoons sugar.
3½ teaspoons baking powder.	1 cup milk.
½ teaspoon salt.	2 tablespoons melted butter.

1 egg.

Mix and bake as One Egg Muffin I.

Twin Mountain Muffins.

¼ cup butter.	¾ cup milk.
¼ cup sugar.	2 cups flour.
1 egg.	3 teaspoons baking powder.

Cream the butter; add sugar and egg well beaten; sift baking powder with flour, and add to the first mixture, alternating with milk. Bake in buttered tin gem pans twenty-five minutes.

Queen of Muffins.

¼ cup butter.	½ cup milk (scant).
⅓ cup sugar.	1½ cups flour.
1 egg.	2½ teaspoons baking powder.

Mix and bake as Twin Mountain Muffins.

Berry Muffins I.   (Without eggs.)

2 cups flour.	2 tablespoons butter.
¼ cup sugar.	1 cup milk (scant).
4 teaspoons baking powder.	1 cup berries.
½ teaspoon salt.	

Mix and sift dry ingredients; work in butter with tips of fingers; add milk and berries.

Berry Muffins II.

¼ cup butter.	4 teaspoons baking powder.
⅓ cup sugar.	½ teaspoon salt.
1 egg.	1 cup milk.
2⅔ cups flour.	1 cup berries.

Cream the butter; add gradually sugar and egg well beaten; mix and sift flour, baking powder, and salt, reserving ¼ cup flour to be mixed with berries and added last; add the remainder alternately with milk.

Rice Muffins.

2½ cups flour.	1 cup milk.
1 cup cooked rice.	1 egg.
4 teaspoons baking powder.	¼ cup melted butter.
½ teaspoon salt.	

Mix and sift flour, salt, and baking powder; work in rice with tips of fingers; add gradually milk, egg well beaten, and butter; bake in buttered muffin rings placed in buttered pan or buttered gem pans.

Oatmeal Muffins.

1 cup cooked oatmeal.	½ teaspoon salt.
1½ cups flour.	½ cup milk.
2 tablespoons sugar.	1 egg.
3 teaspoons baking powder.	1 tablespoon melted butter.

Mix and bake as Rice Muffins.

Quaker Muffins.

⅔ cup rolled oats.	½ teaspoon salt.
1⅓ cups flour.	1 cup scalded milk.
3 tablespoons sugar.	1 egg.
3 teaspoons baking powder.	1 tablespoon melted butter.

Turn scalded milk on rolled oats, let stand five minutes; add sugar, salt, and melted butter; sift in flour and baking powder, mix thoroughly, and add egg well beaten.

Graham Muffins I.

1¼ cups graham flour.	⅓ cup molasses.
1 cup flour.	¾ teaspoon soda.
1 cup sour milk.	1 teaspoon salt.

Mix and sift dry ingredients; add milk to molasses, and combine mixtures.

Graham Muffins II.

1 cup graham or entire wheat flour.	1 teaspoon salt.
1 cup flour.	1 cup milk.
¼ cup sugar.	1 egg.
	1 tablespoon melted butter.
3½ teaspoons baking powder.	

Mix and sift dry ingredients; add milk gradually, egg well beaten, and melted butter; bake in hot oven in buttered gem pans twenty-five minutes.

Rye Muffins I.

Make as Graham Muffins II., substituting rye meal for graham flour.

Rye Muffins II.

1¼ cups rye meal.	¼ cup molasses.
1¼ cups flour.	1¼ cups milk.
4 teaspoons baking powder.	1 egg.
1 teaspoon salt.	1 tablespoon melted butter.

Mix and bake as Graham Muffins II., adding molasses with milk.

Corn Meal Gems.

½ cup corn meal.	1 tablespoon melted butter.
1 cup flour.	½ teaspoon salt.
3 teaspoons baking powder.	¾ cup milk.
1 tablespoon sugar.	1 egg.

Mix and bake as Graham Muffins II.

Berkshire Muffins.

½ cup corn meal.
½ cup flour.
½ cup cooked rice.
2 tablespoons sugar.

½ teaspoon salt.
⅔ cup scalded milk (scant).
1 egg.
1 tablespoon melted butter.

3 teaspoons baking powder.

Turn scalded milk on meal, let stand five minutes; add rice, and flour mixed and sifted with remaining dry ingredients. Add yolk of egg well beaten, butter, and white of egg beaten stiff and dry.

Golden Corn Cake.

¾ cup corn meal.
1¼ cups flour.
¼ cup sugar.
4 teaspoons baking powder.

½ teaspoon salt.
1 cup milk.
1 egg.
1 tablespoon melted butter.

Mix and sift dry ingredients; add milk, egg well beaten, and butter; bake in shallow buttered pan in hot oven twenty minutes.

Corn Cake (sweetened with Molasses).

1 cup corn meal.
¾ cup flour.
3½ teaspoons baking powder.
1 teaspoon salt.

¼ cup molasses.
¾ cup milk.
1 egg.
1 tablespoon melted butter.

Mix and bake as Golden Corn Cake, adding molasses to milk.

White Corn Cake.

¼ cup butter.
½ cup sugar.
1⅓ cups milk.
Whites 3 eggs.

1¼ cups white corn meal.
1¼ cups flour.
4 teaspoons baking powder.
1 teaspoon salt.

Cream the butter; add sugar gradually; add milk, alternating with dry ingredients, mixed and sifted. Beat thoroughly; add whites of eggs beaten stiff. Bake in buttered cake pan thirty minutes.

Susie's Spider Corn Cake.

1½ cups corn meal.	1 teaspoon salt.
2 cups sour milk.	2 eggs.
1 teaspoon soda.	2 tablespoons butter.

Mix soda, salt, and corn meal; gradually add eggs well beaten and milk. Heat frying-pan, grease sides and bottom of pan with butter, turn in the mixture, place on middle grate in hot oven, and cook twenty minutes.

Pop-overs.

1 cup flour.	⅞ cup milk.
¼ teaspoon salt.	1 egg.
½ teaspoon melted butter.	

Mix salt and flour; add milk gradually, in order to obtain a smooth batter. Add egg, beaten until light, and butter; beat two minutes,—using Dover egg-beater, —turn into hissing hot buttered iron gem pans, and bake thirty to thirty-five minutes in a hot oven. They may be baked in buttered earthen cups, when the bottom will have a glazed appearance. Small round iron gem pans are best for Pop-overs.

Graham Pop-overs.

⅔ cup entire wheat flour.	⅞ cup milk.
⅓ cup flour.	1 egg.
¼ teaspoon salt.	½ teaspoon melted butter.

Prepare and bake as Pop-overs.

Breakfast Puffs.

1 cup flour.	½ cup milk.
½ cup water.	

Mix milk and water; add gradually to flour, and beat with Dover egg-beater until very light. Bake as Popovers.

Fadges.

1 cup entire wheat flour.   1 cup cold water.

Add water gradually to flour, and beat with Dover egg-beater until very light.   Bake as Pop-overs.

Maryland Biscuit.

1 pint flour.   1 teaspoon salt.
⅓ cup lard.   Milk and water in equal quantities.
Southern Pupil.

Mix flour and salt; work in lard with tips of fingers, and moisten to a stiff dough.   Toss on slightly floured board, and beat with rolling-pin thirty minutes, continually folding over the dough.   Roll one-third inch in thickness, shape with small round cutter, prick with fork, and place on a buttered tin.   Bake twenty minutes in hot oven.

GRIDDLE-CAKES.

Sour Milk Griddle-Cakes.

2½ cups flour.   2 cups sour milk.
½ teaspoon salt.   1¼ teaspoons soda.
1 egg.

Mix and sift flour, salt, and soda; add sour milk, and egg well beaten.   Drop by spoonfuls on a greased hot griddle; cook on one side.   When puffed, full of bubbles, and cooked on edges, turn, and cook other side.   Serve with butter and maple syrup.

Sweet Milk Griddle-Cakes.

3 cups flour.   ¼ cup sugar.
1½ tablespoons baking powder.   2 cups milk.
1 teaspoon salt.   1 egg.
2 tablespoons melted butter.

Mix and sift dry ingredients; beat egg, add milk, and pour slowly on first mixture.   Beat thoroughly, and add butter.   Cook as Sour Milk Griddle-Cakes.

Entire Wheat Griddle-Cakes.

½ cup entire wheat flour. 3 tablespoons sugar.
1 cup flour. 1 egg.
3 teaspoons baking powder. 1¼ cups milk.
½ teaspoon salt. 1 tablespoon melted butter.

Prepare and cook as Sweet Milk Griddle-Cakes.

Corn Griddle-Cakes.

2 cups flour. ⅓ cup sugar.
½ cup corn meal. 1½ cups boiling water.
1½ tablespoons baking powder. 1¼ cup milk.
1½ teaspoons salt. 1 egg.
2 tablespoons melted butter.

Add meal to boiling water, and boil five minutes; turn into bowl, add milk, and remaining dry ingredients mixed and sifted, then the egg well beaten, and butter. Cook as other griddle-cakes.

Rice Griddle-Cakes I.

2½ cups flour. ¼ cup sugar.
½ cup cold cooked rice. 1½ cups milk.
1 tablespoon baking powder. 1 egg.
½ teaspoon salt. 2 tablespoons melted butter.

Mix and sift dry ingredients. Work in rice with tips of fingers; add egg well beaten, milk, and butter. Cook as other griddle-cakes.

Rice Griddle-Cakes II.

1 cup milk. Yolks 2 eggs.
1 cup warm boiled rice. Whites 2 eggs.
½ teaspoon salt. 1 tablespoon melted butter.
⅞ cup flour.

Pour milk over rice and salt, add yolks of eggs beaten until thick and lemon color, butter, flour, and fold in whites of eggs beaten until stiff and dry.

Bread Griddle-Cakes.

1½ cups fine stale bread crumbs.   2 eggs.
1½ cups scalded milk.   ½ cup flour.
2 tablespoons butter.   ½ teaspoon salt.
        3½ teaspoons baking powder.

Add milk and butter to crumbs, and soak until crumbs
are soft; add eggs well beaten, then flour, salt, and baking powder mixed and sifted.   Cook as other griddle-
cakes.

Buckwheat Cakes.

⅓ cup fine bread crumbs.   ¼ yeast cake.
2 cups scalded milk.   ½ cup lukewarm water.
½ teaspoon salt.   Buckwheat flour.
        1 tablespoon molasses.

Pour milk over crumbs, and soak thirty minutes; add
salt, yeast cake dissolved in lukewarm water, and buckwheat to make a batter thin enough to pour.   Let rise over
night; in the morning, stir well, add molasses, and cook
as griddle-cakes.   Save enough batter to raise another
mixing, instead of using yeast cake; it will require one-
half cup.

Waffles.

2 cups flour.   1 cup milk.
3 teaspoons baking powder.   Yolks 2 eggs.
½ teaspoon salt.   Whites 2 eggs.
        1 tablespoon melted butter.

Mix and sift dry ingredients; add milk gradually, yolks
of eggs well beaten, butter, and whites of eggs beaten
stiff; cook on a greased hot waffle iron.   Serve with maple
syrup.

A waffle iron should fit closely on range, be well heated
on one side, turned, heated on other side, and thoroughly
greased before iron is filled.   In filling, put a tablespoon-
ful of mixture in each compartment near centre of iron,

cover, and mixture will spread to just fill iron. If sufficiently heated, it should be turned almost as soon as filled
and covered. In using a new iron, special care must be
taken in greasing, or waffles will stick.

Rice Waffles.

1¾ cups flour.   3 teaspoons baking powder.
⅔ cup cold cooked rice.   ¼ teaspoon salt.
1½ cups milk.   1 tablespoon melted butter.
2 tablespoons sugar.   1 egg.

Mix and sift dry ingredients; work in rice with tips of
fingers; add milk, yolk of egg well beaten, butter, and
white of egg beaten stiff. Cook as Waffles.

Virginia Waffles.

1½ cups boiling water.   1¼ tablespoons baking powder.
½ cup white corn meal.   1½ teaspoons salt.
1½ cups milk.   Yolks 2 eggs.
2 cups flour.   Whites 2 eggs.
3 tablespoons sugar.   2 tablespoons melted butter.

Cook meal in boiling water twenty minutes; add milk,
dry ingredients mixed and sifted, yolks of eggs well
beaten, butter, and whites of eggs beaten stiff. Cook as
Waffles.

Raised Waffles.

1¾ cups milk.   ¼ cup lukewarm water.
1 teaspoon salt.   2 cups flour.
1 tablespoon butter.   Yolks 2 eggs.
¼ yeast cake.   Whites 2 eggs.

Scald milk; add salt and butter, and when lukewarm,
add yeast cake dissolved in water, and flour. Beat well;
let rise over night; add yolks of eggs well beaten, and
whites of eggs beaten stiff. Cook as Waffles. By using
a whole yeast cake, the mixture will rise in one and
one-half hours.

Fried Drop Cakes.

1⅓ cups flour.	⅓ cup sugar.
2½ teaspoons baking powder.	½ cup milk.
¼ teaspoon salt.	1 egg.

1 teaspoon melted butter.

Beat egg until light; add milk, dry ingredients mixed and sifted, and melted butter. Drop by spoonfuls in hot, new, deep fat; fry until light brown and cooked through, which must at first be determined by piercing with a skewer, or breaking apart. Remove with a skimmer, and drain on brown paper.

Rye Drop Cakes.

⅔ cup rye meal.	½ teaspoon salt.
⅔ cup flour.	2 tablespoons molasses.
2½ teaspoons baking powder.	½ cup milk.

1 egg.

Mix and sift dry ingredients; add milk gradually, molasses, and egg well beaten. Cook as Fried Drop Cakes.

Doughnuts I.

1 cup sugar.	4 teaspoons baking powder.
2½ tablespoons butter.	¼ teaspoon cinnamon.
2 eggs.	¼ teaspoon grated nutmeg.
1 cup milk.	1½ teaspoons salt.

Flour to roll.

Cream the butter, and add one-half sugar. Beat egg until light, add remaining sugar, and combine mixtures. Add three and one-half cups flour, mixed and sifted with baking powder, salt, and spices; then enough more flour to make dough stiff enough to roll. Toss one-third of mixture on floured board, knead slightly, pat, and roll out to one-fourth inch thickness. Shape with a doughnut cutter, fry in deep fat, take up on a skewer, and drain on brown paper. Add trimmings to one-half remaining mixture, roll, shape, and fry as before; repeat. Doughnuts should come quickly to top of fat, brown on one side, then be turned to brown on the other; avoid turning more than once. The fat must be kept at a uniform temperature. If too cold, doughnuts will absorb fat; if too hot, doughnuts will brown before sufficiently risen. See rule for testing fat.

Doughnuts II.

4 cups flour.	¼ teaspoon cinnamon.
1½ teaspoons salt.	½ tablespoon butter.
1¾ teaspoons soda.	1 cup sugar.
1¾ teaspoons cream tartar.	1 cup sour milk.
¼ teaspoon grated nutmeg.	1 egg.

Put flour in shallow pan; add salt, soda, cream tartar, and spices. Work in butter with tips of fingers; add sugar, egg well beaten, and sour milk. Stir thoroughly, and toss on board thickly dredged with flour; knead slightly, using more flour if necessary. Pat and roll out to one-fourth inch thickness; shape, fry, and drain. Sour milk doughnuts may be turned as soon as they come to top of fat, and frequently afterwards.

Raised Doughnuts.

1 cup milk.	⅓ cup butter and lard mixed.
¼ yeast cake.	1 cup light brown sugar.
¼ cup lukewarm water.	2 eggs.
1 teaspoon salt.	½ grated nutmeg.
	Flour.

Scald and cool milk; when lukewarm, add yeast cake dissolved in water, salt, and flour enough to make a stiff batter; let rise over night. In morning add shortening melted, sugar, eggs well beaten, nutmeg, and enough flour to make a stiff dough; let rise again, and if too soft to handle, add more flour. Toss on floured board, pat, and roll to three-fourths inch thickness. Shape with cutter, and work between hands until round. Place on floured board, let rise one hour, turn, and let rise again; fry in deep fat, and drain on brown paper. Cool, and roll in powdered sugar.

Crullers.

¼ cup butter.	4 cups flour.
1 cup sugar.	¼ teaspoon grated nutmeg.
Yolks 2 eggs.	3½ teaspoons baking powder.
Whites 2 eggs.	1 cup milk.

Powdered sugar and cinnamon.

Cream the butter, add sugar gradually, yolks of eggs well beaten, and whites of eggs beaten stiff. Mix flour, nutmeg, and baking powder; add alternately with milk to first mixture; toss on floured board, roll thin, and cut in pieces three inches long by two inches wide; make four one inch gashes at equal intervals. Take up by running finger in and out of gashes, and lower into deep fat. Fry same as Doughnuts I.

Strawberry Short Cake I.

2 cups flour.	2 teaspoons sugar.
4 teaspoons baking powder.	¾ cup milk.
½ teaspoon salt.	¼ cup butter.

Mix dry ingredients, sift twice, work in butter with tips of fingers, and add milk gradually. Toss on floured board, divide in two parts. Pat, roll out, and bake twelve minutes in a hot oven in buttered Washington pie or round layer cake tins. Split and spread with butter. Sweeten strawberries to taste, place on back of range until warmed, crush slightly, and put between and on top of Short Cakes; cover top with Cream Sauce I. Allow from one to one and one-half boxes berries to each Short Cake.

Strawberry Short Cake II.

2 cups flour.	1 tablespoon sugar.
4 teaspoons baking powder.	¾ cup milk.
½ teaspoon salt.	⅓ cup butter.

Mix as Strawberry Short Cake I. Toss and roll on floured board. Put in round buttered tin, and shape with back of hand to fit pan.

Rich Strawberry Short Cake.

2 cups flour.
¼ cup sugar.
4 teaspoons baking powder.
½ teaspoon salt.

Few grains nutmeg.
1 egg.
⅓ cup butter.
1¼ tablespoons lard.

⅓ cup milk.

Hotel Pastry Cook.

Mix dry ingredients and sift twice, work in shortening
with tips of fingers, add egg well beaten, and milk. Bake
as Strawberry Short Cake II. Split cake and spread under
layer with Cream Sauce II. Cover with strawberries which
have been sprinkled with powdered sugar; again spread
with sauce, and cover with upper layer.

Fruit Short Cake.

¼ cup butter.
½ cup sugar.
1 egg.

¼ cup milk.
1 cup flour.
2 teaspoons baking powder.

¼ teaspoon salt.

Cream the butter, add sugar gradually, and egg well
beaten. Mix and sift flour, baking powder, and salt, adding alternately with milk to first mixture. Beat thoroughly, and bake in a buttered round tin. Cool, spread
thickly with sweetened fruit, and cover with Cream Sauce
I. or II. Fresh strawberries, peaches, apricots, raspberries, or canned quince or pineapple may be used.
When canned goods are used, drain fruit from syrup and
cut in pieces. Dilute cream for Cream Sauce with fruit
syrup in place of milk.

CHAPTER III.

HOT PUDDINGS.

Rice Pudding.

4 cups milk.	½ teaspoon salt.
⅓ cup rice.	⅓ cup sugar.

Grated rind ½ lemon.

Wash rice, mix ingredients, and pour into buttered pudding-dish; bake three hours in very slow oven, stirring three times during first hour of baking to prevent rice from settling.

Poor Man's Pudding.

4 cups milk.	½ teaspoon salt.
½ cup rice.	½ teaspoon cinnamon.
⅓ cup molasses.	1 tablespoon butter.

Wash rice, mix and bake same as Rice Pudding. At last stirring, add butter.

Indian Pudding.

5 cups scalded milk.	½ cup molasses.
⅓ cup Indian meal.	1 teaspoon salt.

1 teaspoon ginger.

Pour milk slowly on meal, cook in double boiler twenty minutes, add molasses, salt, and ginger; pour into buttered pudding-dish and bake two hours in slow oven; serve with cream. If baked too rapidly it will not whey. Ginger may be omitted.

Cerealine Pudding (Mock Indian).

4 cups scalded milk.	½ cup molasses.
2 cups cerealine.	1½ teaspoons salt.

1½ tablespoons butter.

Pour milk on cerealine, add remaining ingredients, pour into buttered pudding-dish, and bake one hour in slow oven. Serve with cream.

Apple Tapioca.

¾ cup pearl or Minute Tapioca.	½ teaspoon salt.
Cold water.	7 sour apples.
2½ cups boiling water.	½ cup sugar.

Soak tapioca one hour in cold water to cover, drain, add boiling water and salt; cook in double boiler until transparent. Core and pare apples, arrange in buttered pudding-dish, fill cavities with sugar, pour over tapioca, and bake in moderate oven until apples are soft. Serve with sugar and cream or Cream Sauce I. Minute Tapioca requires no soaking.

Tapioca Custard Pudding.

4 cups scalded milk.	½ cup sugar.
⅔ cup pearl tapioca.	1 teaspoon salt.
3 eggs.	1 tablespoon butter.

Soak tapioca one hour in cold water to cover, drain, add to milk, and cook in double boiler thirty minutes; beat eggs slightly, add sugar and salt, pour on gradually hot mixture, turn into buttered pudding-dish, add butter, bake thirty minutes in slow oven.

Peach Tapioca.

1 can peaches.	Boiling water.
¼ cup powdered sugar.	½ cup sugar.
1 cup tapioca.	½ teaspoon salt.

Drain peaches, sprinkle with powdered sugar, and let stand one hour; soak tapioca one hour in cold water to cover; to peach syrup add enough boiling water to make three cups; heat to boiling point, add tapioca drained from cold water, sugar, and salt; then cook in double boiler until transparent. Line a mould or pudding-dish with peaches cut in quarters, fill with tapioca, and bake in moderate oven thirty minutes; cool slightly, turn on a dish, and serve with Cream Sauce I.

Scalloped Apples.

1 small stale baker's loaf.	¼ cup sugar.
¼ cup butter.	¼ teaspoon grated nutmeg.
1 quart sliced apples.	Grated rind and juice of ½ lemon.

Cut loaf in halves, remove soft part, and crumb by rubbing through a colander; melt butter and stir in lightly with fork; cover bottom of buttered pudding-dish with crumbs and spread over one-half the apples, sprinkle with one-half sugar, nutmeg, lemon juice and rind mixed together; repeat, cover with remaining crumbs, and bake forty minutes in moderate oven. Cover at first to prevent crumbs browning too rapidly. Serve with sugar and cream.

Bread Pudding.

2 cups stale bread crumbs.	2 eggs.
1 quart scalded milk.	½ teaspoon salt.
⅓ cup sugar.	1 teaspoon vanilla or
¼ cup melted butter.	¼ teaspoon spice.

Soak bread crumbs in milk, set aside until cool; add sugar, butter, eggs slightly beaten, salt, and flavoring; bake one hour in buttered budding-dish in slow oven; serve with Vanilla Sauce. In preparing bread crumbs for puddings avoid using outside crusts. With a coarse grater there need be but little waste.

Cracker Custard Pudding.

Make same as Bread Pudding, using two-thirds cup cracker crumbs in place of bread crumbs; after baking, cover with meringue made of whites two eggs, one-fourth cup powdered sugar, and one tablespoon lemon juice; return to oven to cook meringue.

Bread and Butter Pudding.

1 small stale baker's loaf.	½ cup sugar.
Butter.	¼ teaspoon salt.
3 eggs.	1 quart milk.

Remove end crusts from bread, cut loaf in one-half inch slices, spread each slice generously with butter; arrange in buttered pudding-dish, buttered side down. Beat eggs slightly, add sugar, salt, and milk; strain, and pour over bread; let stand thirty minutes. Bake one hour in slow oven, covering the first half-hour of baking. The top of pudding should be well browned. Serve with Hard or Creamy Sauce. Three-fourths cup raisins, parboiled in boiling water to cover, and seeded, may be sprinkled between layers of bread.

Chocolate Bread Pudding.

2 cups stale bread crumbs.	⅔ cup sugar.
4 cups scalded milk.	2 eggs.
2 squares Baker's chocolate.	¼ teaspoon salt.
1 teaspoon vanilla.	

Soak bread in milk thirty minutes; melt chocolate in saucepan placed over hot water, add one-half sugar and enough milk taken from bread and milk to make of consistency to pour; add to mixture with remaining sugar, salt, vanilla, and eggs slightly beaten; turn into buttered pudding-dish and bake one hour in a moderate oven. Serve with Hard or Cream Sauce I.

Cottage Pudding.

¼ cup butter.	1 cup milk.
½ cup sugar.	2 cups flour.
1 egg.	3 teaspoons baking powder.
½ teaspoon salt.	

Cream the butter, add sugar gradually, and egg well beaten; mix and sift flour, baking powder, and salt; add alternately with milk to first mixture; turn into buttered cake-pan; bake thirty-five minutes. Serve with Vanilla or Hard Sauce.

Strawberry Cottage Pudding.

⅓ cup butter.	½ cup milk.
1 cup sugar.	1¾ cups flour.
1 egg.	3 teaspoons baking powder.

Mix same as Cottage Pudding, and bake twenty-five minutes in shallow pan; cut in squares and serve with strawberries (sprinkled with sugar and slightly mashed) and Cream Sauce I. *Sliced peaches* may be used in place of strawberries.

Orange Puffs.

⅓ cup butter.	½ cup milk.
1 cup sugar.	1¾ cups flour.
2 eggs.	3 teaspoons baking powder.

Mix same as Cottage Pudding, and bake in buttered individual tins. Serve with Orange Sauce.

Custard Soufflé.

3 tablespoons butter.	1 cup scalded milk.
¼ cup flour.	4 eggs.
¼ cup sugar.	

Melt butter, add flour, and gradually hot milk; when well thickened, pour on to yolks of eggs beaten until thick and lemon colored, and mixed with sugar; cool, and cut and fold in whites of eggs beaten stiff and dry. Turn into buttered pudding-dish, and bake from thirty to thirty-five minutes in slow oven; take from oven and serve at once, — if not served immediately it is sure to fall; serve with Creamy or Foamy Sauce.

Lemon Soufflé.

Yolks 4 eggs.   1 cup sugar.
Grated rind and juice 1 lemon.   Whites 4 eggs.

Beat yolks until thick and lemon colored, add sugar gradually and continue beating, then add lemon rind and juice. Cut and fold in whites of eggs beaten until dry; turn into buttered pudding-dish, set in pan of hot water, and bake thirty-five to forty minutes. Serve with or without sauce.

Fruit Soufflé.

¾ cup fruit pulp, peach,   Whites 3 eggs.
   apricot, or quince.   Sugar.

Rub fruit through sieve; if canned fruit is used, first drain from syrup. Heat and sweeten if needed; beat whites of eggs until stiff, add gradually hot fruit pulp, and continue beating; turn into buttered and sugared individual moulds, having them three-fourths full; set moulds in pan of hot water and bake in slow oven until firm, which may be determined by pressing with finger; serve with Sabyon Sauce.

Spanish Soufflé.

¼ cup butter.   2 tablespoons sugar.
½ cup stale bread crumbs.   3 eggs.
1 cup milk.   ½ teaspoon vanilla.

Melt butter, add crumbs, cook until slightly browned, stirring often; add milk and sugar, cook twenty minutes in double boiler; remove from fire, add unbeaten yolks of eggs, then cut and fold in whites of eggs beaten until stiff, and flavor. Bake as Fruit Soufflé.

Chestnut Soufflé.

¼ cup sugar.   1 cup chestnut purée.
2 tablespoons flour.   ½ cup milk.
              Whites 3 eggs.

Mix sugar and flour, add chestnuts and milk gradually; cook five minutes, stirring constantly; beat whites of eggs

until stiff, and cut and fold into mixture.   Bake as Fruit
Soufflé; serve with Cream Sauce.

Steamed Apple Pudding.

2 cups flour.	2 tablespoons butter.
4 teaspoons baking powder.	¾ cup milk.
½ teaspoon salt.	4 apples cut in eighths.

Mix and sift dry ingredients; work in butter with tips
of fingers, add milk gradually, mixing with a knife; toss
on floured board, pat and roll out, place apples on middle
of dough, and sprinkle with one tablespoon sugar mixed
with one-fourth teaspoon each of salt and nutmeg; bring
dough around apples and carefully lift into buttered mould
or five-pound lard pail; or apples may be sprinkled over
dough, and dough rolled like a jelly roll; cover closely
and steam one hour and twenty minutes; serve with Vanilla or Cold Sauce.   Twice the number of apples may
be sprinkled with sugar and cooked until soft in granite
kettle placed on top of range, covered with dough, rolled
size to fit in kettle, then kettle covered tightly and dough
steamed fifteen minutes.   When turned on dish for serving, apples will be on top.

Steamed Blueberry Pudding.

Mix and sift dry ingredients and work in butter same
as for Steamed Apple Pudding.   Add one cup each of
milk, and blueberries rolled in flour; turn into buttered
mould and steam one and one-half hours.   Serve with
Creamy Sauce.

Steamed Cranberry Pudding.

½ cup butter.	3½ cups flour.
1 cup sugar.	1¼ tablespoons baking powder.
3 eggs.	½ cup milk.
1½ cups cranberries.	

Cream the butter, add sugar gradually, and eggs well
beaten.   Mix and sift flour and baking powder and add

alternately with milk to first mixture, stir in berries previously washed, turn into buttered mould, cover, and steam three hours. Serve with thin cream, sweetened and flavored with nutmeg.

Ginger Pudding.

⅓ cup butter.	3½ teaspoons baking powder.
½ cup sugar.	¼ teaspoon salt.
1 egg.	2 teaspoons ginger.
2¼ cups flour.	1 cup milk.

Cream the butter, add sugar gradually, and egg well beaten; mix and sift dry ingredients; add alternately with milk to first mixture. Turn into buttered mould, cover, and steam two hours; serve with Vanilla Sauce.

Harvard Pudding.

⅓ cup butter.	3½ teaspoons baking powder.
½ cup sugar.	¼ teaspoon salt.
2½ cups flour.	1 egg.

1 cup milk.

Mix and sift dry ingredients and work in butter with tips of fingers; beat egg, add milk, and combine mixtures; turn into buttered mould, cover, and steam two hours; serve with warm apple sauce and Hard Sauce.

Apple Sauce. Pick over and wash dried apples, soak over night in cold water to cover; cook until soft; sweeten, and flavor with lemon juice.

Swiss Pudding.

½ cup butter.	Grated rind one lemon.
⅞ cup flour.	5 eggs.
2 cups milk.	⅓ cup powdered sugar.

Cream the butter, add flour gradually; scald milk with lemon rind, add to first mixture, and cook five minutes in double boiler. Beat yolks of eggs until thick and lemon colored, add sugar gradually, then add to cooked mixture; cool, and cut and fold in whites of eggs beaten stiff. Turn into buttered mould, cover, and steam one and one-fourth hours; while steaming, be sure water surrounds mould to half its depth.

Snow Balls.

½ cup butter.	2¼ cups flour.
1 cup sugar.	3½ teaspoons baking powder.
½ cup milk.	Whites 4 eggs.

Cream the butter, add sugar gradually, milk, and flour mixed and sifted with baking powder; then add the whites of eggs beaten stiff. Steam thirty-five minutes in buttered cups; serve with preserved fruit, quince marmalade, or strawberry sauce.

Graham Pudding.

¼ cup butter.	1½ cups Graham flour.
½ cup molasses.	½ teaspoon soda.
½ cup milk.	1 teaspoon salt.
1 egg.	1 cup raisins seeded and cut in pieces.

Melt butter, add molasses, milk, egg well beaten, dry ingredients mixed and sifted, and raisins; turn into buttered mould, cover, and steam two and one-half hours. Serve with Wine Sauce. Dates or figs cut in small pieces may be used in place of raisins.

St. James Pudding.

3 tablespoons butter.	Salt,
½ cup molasses.	Clove,
½ cup milk.	Allspice, } ¼ teaspoon each.
1⅔ cups flour.	Nutmeg,
½ teaspoon soda.	½ lb. dates stoned and cut in pieces.

Mix and steam same as Graham Pudding. A simple, delicious pudding without egg. Puddings may be nicely steamed in buttered one-pound baking-powder boxes, and are attractive in shape and easy to serve.

Suet Pudding.

1 cup finely chopped suet.	1½ teaspoons salt.
1 cup molasses.	Ginger,
1 cup milk.	Clove, ⎫ ½ teaspoon each.
3 cups flour.	Nutmeg, ⎭
1 teaspoon soda.	1 teaspoon cinnamon.

Mix and sift dry ingredients. Add molasses and milk to suet; combine mixtures. Turn into buttered mould, cover, and steam three hours; serve with Egg Sauce. Raisins and currants may be added.

Thanksgiving Pudding.

4 cups scalded milk.	⅓ cup melted butter.
1¼ cups rolled crackers.	½ grated nutmeg.
1 cup sugar.	1 teaspoon salt.
4 eggs.	1½ cups raisins.

Pour milk over crackers and let stand until cool; add sugar, eggs slightly beaten, nutmeg, salt, and butter; parboil raisins until soft, by cooking in boiling water to cover; seed, and add to mixture; turn into buttered pudding-dish and bake slowly two and one-half hours, stirring after first half-hour to prevent raisins from settling; serve with Brandy Sauce.

Hunters' Pudding.

1 cup finely chopped suet.	Clove,
1 cup molasses.	Mace, ⎫ ½ teaspoon each.
1 cup milk.	Allspice, ⎭
3 cups flour.	1 teaspoon cinnamon.
1 teaspoon soda.	1½ cups raisins.
1½ teaspoons salt.	2 tablespoons flour.

Mix same as Suet Pudding. Stone, cut, and flour raisins, then add to mixture. Turn into buttered mould, cover, and steam three hours.

French Fruit Pudding.

1 cup finely chopped suet.	½ teaspoon clove.
1 cup molasses.	½ teaspoon salt.
1 cup sour milk.	1¼ cups raisins seeded
1½ teaspoons soda.	and chopped.
1 teaspoon cinnamon.	¾ cup currants.

2½ cups flower.

Mrs. Carrie M. Dearborn.

Add molasses and sour milk to suet; add two cups
flour mixed and sifted with soda, salt, and spices; add
fruit mixed with remaining flour.   Turn into buttered
mould, cover, and steam four hours.   Serve with Sterling
Sauce.

English Plum Pudding.

½ lb. stale bread crumbs.	2 oz. finely cut citron.
1 cup scalded milk.	½ lb. suet.
¼ lb. sugar.	¼ cup wine and brandy mixed.
4 eggs.	½ grated nutmeg.
½ lb. raisins, seeded, cut	¾ teaspoon cinnamon.
in pieces, and floured.	⅓ teaspoon clove.
¼ lb. currants.	⅓ teaspoon mace.
¼ lb. finely chopped figs.	1½ teaspoons salt.

Soak bread crumbs in milk, let stand until cool, add
sugar, beaten yolks of eggs, raisins, currants, figs, and
citron; chop suet, and cream by using the hand; combine mixtures, then add wine, brandy, nutmeg, cinnamon,
clove, mace, and whites of eggs beaten stiff.   Turn into
buttered mould, cover, and steam six hours.

Fig Pudding.

⅓ lb. beef suet.	½ cup milk.
½ lb. figs, finely chopped.	2 eggs.
2⅓ cups stale bread crumbs.	1 cup sugar.

¾ teaspoon salt.

Chop suet, and work with the hands until creamy, then
add figs.   Soak bread crumbs in milk, add eggs well
beaten, sugar, and salt.   Combine mixtures, turn into a
buttered mould, steam three hours.   Serve with Yellow
Sauce I. or II.

CHAPTER IV.

COLD DESSERTS.

Irish Moss Blanc-Mange.

⅓ cup Irish moss.   ¼ teaspoon salt.
4 cups milk.   1½ teaspoons vanilla.

Soak moss fifteen minutes in cold water to cover, drain, pick over, and add to milk; cook in double boiler thirty minutes; the milk will seem but little thicker than when put on to cook, but if cooked longer blanc-mange will be too stiff.   Add salt, strain, flavor, re-strain, and fill individual moulds previously dipped in cold water; chill, turn on glass dish, surround with thin slices of banana, and place a slice on each mould.   Serve with sugar and cream.

Chocolate Blanc-Mange.

Irish Moss Blanc-Mange flavored with chocolate.   Melt one and one-half squares Baker's chocolate, add one-fourth cup sugar and one-third cup boiling water, stir until perfectly smooth, adding to milk just before taking from fire. Serve with sugar and cream.

Rebecca Pudding.

4 cups scalded milk.   ¼ teaspoon salt.
½ cup corn-starch.   ½ cup cold milk.
¼ cup sugar.   1 teaspoon vanilla.
                Whites 3 eggs.

Mix corn-starch, sugar, and salt, dilute with cold milk, add to scalded milk, stirring constantly until mixture

thickens, afterwards occasionally; cook fifteen minutes.
Add flavoring and whites of eggs beaten stiff, mix thoroughly, mould, chill, and serve with Yellow Sauce I. or II.

Moulded Snow.

Make as Rebecca Pudding, and serve with Chocolate
Sauce.

Chocolate Cream.

2 cups scalded milk.	⅓ cup cold milk.
5 tablespoons corn-starch.	1½ squares Baker's chocolate.
½ cup sugar.	3 tablespoons hot water.
¼ teaspoon salt.	Whites 3 eggs.

1 teaspoon vanilla.

Mix corn-starch, sugar, and salt, dilute with cold milk,
add to scalded milk, and cook over hot water ten minutes,
stirring constantly until thickened; melt chocolate, add
hot water, stir until smooth, and add to cooked mixture;
add whites of eggs beaten stiff, and vanilla. Mould,
chill, and serve with cream.

Pineapple Pudding.

2¾ cups scalded milk.	¼ cup sugar.
¼ cup cold milk.	¼ teaspoon salt.
⅓ cup corn-starch.	½ can grated pineapple.

Whites 3 eggs.

Follow directions for Rebecca Pudding, and add pineapple just before moulding. Fill individual moulds, previously dipped in cold water. Serve with cream.

Boiled Custard.

2 cups scalded milk.	¼ cup sugar.
Yolks 3 eggs.	⅛ teaspoon salt.

½ teaspoon vanilla.

Beat eggs slightly, add sugar and salt; stir constantly
while adding gradually hot milk. Cook in double boiler,
continue stirring until mixture thickens and a coating is

formed on the spoon, strain immediately; chill and flavor. If cooked too long the custard will curdle; should this happen, by using a Dover egg-beater it may be restored to a smooth consistency, but custard will not be as thick. Eggs should be beaten slightly for custard, that it may be of smooth, thick consistency. To prevent scum from forming, cover with a perforated tin. When eggs are scarce, use yolks two eggs and one-half tablespoon corn-starch.

Tipsy Pudding.

Flavor Boiled Custard with sherry wine, and pour over slices of stale sponge cake; cover with Cream Sauce I. or II.

Peach Custard.

Arrange alternate layers of stale cake and sections of canned peaches in glass dish and pour over Boiled Custard. Bananas may be used instead of peaches; it is then called *Banana Custard*.

Orange Custard.

Arrange slices of sweet oranges in glass dish, pour over them Boiled Custard; chill, and cover with Meringue I.

Apple Meringue.

Use Meringue I. and pile lightly on baked apples, brown in oven, cool, and serve with Boiled Custard. Canned peaches, drained from their liquor, may be prepared in the same way; it is then called *Peach Meringue*.

Apple Snow.

Whites 3 eggs. ¾ cup apple pulp.
Powdered sugar.

Pare, quarter, and core four sour apples, steam until soft, and rub through sieve; there should be three-fourths cup apple pulp. Beat on a platter whites of eggs until stiff (using wire whisk), add gradually apple sweetened to taste, and continue beating. Pile lightly on glass dish, chill, and serve with Boiled Custard.

Prune Whip.

| ⅓ lb. prunes. | ½ cup sugar. |
| Whites 5 eggs. | ½ tablespoon lemon juice. |

Pick over and wash prunes, then soak several hours in cold water to cover; cook in same water until soft; remove stones and rub prunes through a strainer, add sugar, and cook five minutes; the mixture should be of the consistency of marmalade. Beat whites of eggs until stiff, add prune mixture gradually when cold, and lemon juice. Pile lightly on buttered pudding-dish, bake twenty minutes in slow oven. Serve cold with Boiled Custard.

Raspberry Whip.

| 1¼ cups raspberries. | 1 cup powdered sugar. |
| | White 1 egg. |

Put ingredients in bowl and beat with wire whisk until stiff enough to hold in shape; about thirty minutes will be required for beating. Pile lightly on dish, chill, surround with lady fingers, and serve with Boiled Custard.

Strawberry Whip may be prepared in same way.

Baked Custard.

4 cups scalded milk.	½ cup sugar.
4 to 6 eggs.	¼ teaspoon salt.
	Few gratings nutmeg.

Beat eggs slightly, add sugar and salt, pour on slowly scalded milk; strain in buttered mould, set in pan of hot water. Sprinkle with nutmeg, and bake in slow oven until firm, which may be readily determined by running a silver knife through custard; if knife comes out clean, custard is done. During baking, care must be taken that water surrounding mould does not reach boiling point, or custard will whey. Always bear in mind that eggs and milk in combination must be cooked at a low temperature. For *cup custards* allow four eggs to four cups milk; for large moulded custard, six eggs; if less eggs are used custard is liable to crack when turned on a serving-dish.

Caramel Custard.

4 cups scalded milk.	½ teaspoon salt.
5 eggs.	1 teaspoon vanilla.
	½ cup sugar.

Put sugar in omelet pan, stir constantly over hot part of range until melted to a syrup of light brown color. Add gradually to milk, being careful that milk does not bubble up and go over, as is liable on account of high temperature of sugar. As soon as sugar is melted in milk, add mixture gradually to eggs slightly beaten; add salt and flavoring, then strain in buttered mould. Bake as custard. Chill, and serve with Caramel Sauce.

Caramel Sauce.

½ cup sugar.	½ cup boiling water.

Miss Parloa.

Melt sugar as for Caramel Custard, add water, simmer ten minutes; cool before serving.

Tapioca Cream.

¼ cup pearl tapioca or 2 table-spoons Minute Tapioca.	2 eggs.
	⅓ cup sugar.
2 cups scalded milk.	¼ teaspoon salt.
1 teaspoon vanilla.	

Pick over tapioca and soak one hour in cold water to cover, drain, add to milk, and cook in double boiler until tapioca is transparent. Add half the sugar to milk and remainder to egg yolks slightly beaten, and salt. Combine by pouring hot mixture slowly on egg mixture, return to double boiler, and cook until it thickens. Remove from range and add whites of eggs beaten stiff. Chill and flavor.

Norwegian Prune Pudding.

½ lb. prunes.   1 inch piece stick cinnamon.
2 cups cold water.   1 cup boiling water.
1 cup sugar.   ⅓ cup corn-starch.

Pick over and wash prunes, then soak one hour in cold water, and boil until soft; remove stones, obtain meat from stones and add to prunes; then add sugar, cinnamon, boiling water, and simmer ten minutes. Dilute corn-starch with enough cold water to pour easily, add to prune mixture, and cook eight minutes in double boiler. Remove cinnamon, mould, then chill, and serve with Cream Sauce I. or II.

Apples in Bloom.

Select eight red apples, cook in boiling water until soft, turning them often. Have water half surround apples. Remove skins carefully, that the red color may remain, and arrange on serving-dish. To the water add one cup sugar, grated rind one-half lemon, and juice one orange; simmer until reduced to one cup. Cool, and pour over apples. Serve with Cream Sauce I. or II.

Neapolitan Baskets.

Bake sponge cake in gem pans, cool, and remove centres. Fill with Cream Sauce II., flavoring half the sauce with chocolate. Melt chocolate, dilute with hot water, cool, and add cream sauce slowly to chocolate. Garnish with candied cherries and angelica.

Wine Cream.

Arrange lady fingers or slices of sponge cake in a dish, pour over cream made as follows: Mix one-third cup sugar, grated rind and juice one-half lemon, one-fourth cup sherry wine, and yolks of two eggs; place over fire and stir vigorously with wire whisk until it thickens and is frothy, then pour over beaten whites of two eggs and continue beating

Orange Salad.

Arrange layers of sliced oranges, sprinkling each layer with powdered sugar and shredded cocoanut. Sliced oranges when served alone should not stand long after slicing, as they are apt to become bitter.

Fruit Salad I.

Arrange alternate layers of shredded pineapple, sliced bananas, and sliced oranges, sprinkling each layer with powdered sugar. Chill before serving.

To Shred Pineapple. Pare and cut out eyes, pick off small pieces with a silver fork, continuing until all soft part is removed. *To Slice Oranges.* Remove skin and white covering, slice lengthwise that the tough centre may not be served; seeds should be removed.

Fruit Salad II.

Pare a pineapple and cut in one-quarter inch slices, remove hard centres, sprinkle with powdered sugar, set aside one hour in a cool place; drain, spread on serving-dish, arrange a circle of thin slices of banana on each piece, nearly to the edge, pile strawberries in centre, pour over syrup drained from pineapple, sprinkle with powdered sugar, and serve with or without Cream Sauce.

Fruit Salad with Wine Dressing.

Arrange alternate layers of sliced fruit, using pineapples, bananas, oranges, and grapes; pour over all Wine Dressing, and let stand one hour in a cold place.

Wine Dressing.

Mix one-half cup sugar, one-third cup sherry wine, and two tablespoons Madeira.

Cream Whips.

Sweeten thin cream, flavor with vanilla, brandy, or wine, then whip; half fill frappé glasses with any preserve, pile on lightly the whip.

Lemon Jelly.

½ box gelatine or
2 tablespoons granulated gelatine.

½ cup cold water.
2½ cups boiling water.
1 cup sugar.

½ cup lemon juice.

Soak gelatine twenty minutes in cold water, dissolve in boiling water, strain, and add to sugar and lemon juice. Turn into mould, and chill.

Orange Jelly.

½ box gelatine or
2 tablespoons granulated gelatine.
½ cup cold water.

1½ cups boiling water.
1 cup sugar.
1½ cups orange juice.
3 tablespoons lemon juice.

Make same as Lemon Jelly.

To Remove Juice from Oranges. Cut fruit in halves crosswise, remove with spoon pulp and juice from sections, and strain through double cheese cloth; or use a glass lemon squeezer.

Coffee Jelly.

½ box gelatine or
2 tablespoons granulated gelatine.

½ cup cold water.
1 cup boiling water.
⅓ cup sugar.

2 cups boiled coffee.

Make same as Lemon Jelly. Serve with sugar and cream.

Cider Jelly.

½ box gelatine or
2 tablespoons granulated gelatine.

½ cup cold water.
1 cup boiling water.
2 cups cider.

Make same as Lemon Jelly.

Wine Jelly I.

½ box gelatine or	1 cup sugar.
2 tablespoons granulated gelatine.	1 cup sherry or Madeira wine.
½ cup cold water.	⅓ cup orange juice.
1⅔ cups boiling water.	3 tablespoons lemon juice.

Soak gelatine twenty minutes in cold water, dissolve in boiling water; add sugar, wine, orange juice, and lemon juice; strain, mould, and chill. If a stronger jelly is desired, use additional wine in place of orange juice.

Wine Jelly II.

½ box gelatine or	½ cup sherry wine.
2½ tablespoons granulated gelatine.	2 tablespoons brandy.
	Kirsch.
½ cup cold water.	⅓ cup orange juice.
1⅔ cups boiling water.	3 tablespoons lemon juice.
1 cup sugar.	Fruit red.

Soak gelatine twenty minutes in cold water, dissolve in hot water, add sugar, fruit juices, sherry, brandy, and enough Kirsch to make one cup of strong liquor, then color with fruit red. Strain, mould, and chill.

Russian Jelly.

¼ box gelatine or	1 cup boiling water.
1 tablespoon granulated gelatine.	⅔ cup sugar.
	½ cup Sauterne.
¼ cup cold water.	¼ cup orange juice.
1½ tablespoons lemon juice.	

Make same as other jellies, cool, and beat until frothy and firm enough to mould.

Jelly in Glasses.

Use recipe for Wine or Russian Jelly. Fill Apollinaris glasses three-fourths full, reserving one-fourth of the mixture, which, after cooling, is to be beaten until frothy and placed on top of jelly in glasses. This is a most attractive way of serving jelly to one who is ill.

Jellied Prunes.

⅓ lb. prunes.
2 cups cold water.
Boiling water.
½ cup cold water.

½ box gelatine or
2½ tablespoons granulated
gelatine.
1 cup sugar.

¼ cup lemon juice.

Pick over, wash, and soak prunes for several hours in two cups cold water, and cook in same water until soft; remove prunes; stone, and cut in quarters. To prune water add enough boiling water to make two cups. Soak gelatine in half-cup cold water, dissolve in hot liquid, add sugar, lemon juice, then strain, add prunes, mould, and chill. Stir twice while cooling to prevent prunes from settling. Serve with sugar and cream.

Jellied Walnuts.

¼ box gelatine or
1 tablespoon granulated
gelatine.
¼ cup cold water.

⅓ cup boiling water.
¾ cup sugar.
½ cup sherry wine.
½ cup orange juice.

3 tablespoons lemon juice.

Make same as other jellies and cover bottom of shallow pan with mixture. When firm, place over it, one inch apart, halves of English walnuts. Cover with remaining mixture. Chill, and cut in squares for serving.

Apricot and Wine Jelly.

½ box gelatine or
2 tablespoons granulated
gelatine.
½ cup cold water.

1 cup boiling water.
1 cup apricot juice.
1 cup wine.
1 cup sugar.

1 tablespoon lemon juice.

Garnish individual moulds with halves of apricots, fill with mixture made same as for other jellies, and chill. Serve with Cream Sauce I.

Snow Pudding I.

¼ box gelatine or
1 tablespoon granulated gelatine.
¼ cup cold water.

1 cup boiling water.
1 cup sugar.
¼ cup lemon juice.

Whites 3 eggs.

Soak gelatine in cold water, dissolve in boiling water, add sugar and lemon juice, strain, and set aside in cool place; occasionally stir mixture, and when quite thick, beat with wire spoon or whisk until frothy; add whites of eggs beaten stiff, and continue beating until stiff enough to hold its shape. Mould, or pile by spoonfuls on glass dish; serve cold with Boiled Custard. A very attractive dish may be prepared by coloring half the mixture with fruit red.

Amber Pudding.

Make as Snow Pudding I., using cider instead of boiling water, and one-fourth cup boiling water to dissolve gelatine, omitting lemon juice, and sweeten to taste.

Snow Pudding II.

Beat whites of four eggs until stiff, add one-half tablespoon granulated gelatine dissolved in three tablespoons boiling water, beat until thoroughly mixed, add one-fourth cup powdered sugar, and flavor with one-half teaspoon lemon extract. Pile lightly on dish, serve with Boiled Custard.

Pudding à la Macédoine.

Make fruit or wine jelly mixture. Place a mould in pan of ice water, pour in mixture one-half inch deep; when firm, decorate with slices of banana from which radiate thin strips of figs (seed side down), cover fruit, adding mixture by spoonfuls lest the fruit be disarranged. When firm, add more fruit and mixture; repeat until all is used, each time allowing mixture to stiffen before fruit

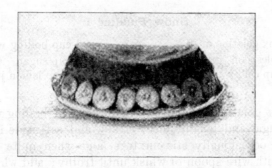

Pudding à la Macédoine.

is added. In preparing this dish various fruits may be used: oranges, bananas, dates, figs, and English walnuts. Serve with Cream Sauce I.

Fruit Chartreuse.

Make fruit or wine jelly mixture. Place a mould in pan of ice water, pour in mixture one-half inch deep; when firm, decorate with candied cherries and angelica; add by spoonfuls more mixture to cover fruit; when this is firm, place a smaller mould in the centre on jelly, and fill with ice water. Pour gradually remaining jelly mixture between moulds; when firm, invert to empty smaller mould of ice water; then pour in some tepid water; let stand a few seconds, when small mould may easily be removed. Fill space thus made with fresh sweetened fruit, using shredded pineapple, sliced bananas, and strawberries.

Spanish Cream.

¼ box gelatine or
1 tablespoon granulated
    gelatine.
3 cups milk.
Whites 3 eggs.

Yolks 3 eggs.
½ cup sugar (scant).
¼ teaspoon salt.
1 teaspoon vanilla or
3 tablespoons wine.

Scald milk with gelatine, add sugar, pour slowly on yolks of eggs slightly beaten. Return to double boiler and cook until thickened, stirring constantly; remove from range, add salt, flavoring, and whites of eggs beaten stiff. Turn into individual moulds, first dipped in cold water, and chill; serve with cream. More gelatine will be required if large moulds are used.

Columbian Pudding.

Cover the bottom of a fancy mould with Wine Jelly. Line the upper part of mould with figs, cut in halves cross-wise, which have been soaked in jelly, having seed side next to mould. Fill centre with Spanish Cream; chill, and turn on a serving dish. Garnish with cubes of Wine Jelly.

Macaroon Cream.

¼ box gelatine or
1 tablespoon granulated
   gelatine.
¼ cup cold water.
2 cups scalded milk.

Yolks 3 eggs.
⅓ cup sugar.
⅛ teaspoon salt.
⅔ cup pounded macaroons.
1 teaspoon vanilla.

Whites 3 eggs.

Soak gelatine in cold water. Make custard of milk, yolks of eggs, sugar, and salt; add soaked gelatine; when dissolved, strain into pan set in ice water. Add macaroons and flavoring, stirring until it begins to thicken; then add whites of eggs beaten stiff, mould, chill, and serve garnished with macaroons.

Cold Cabinet Pudding.

¼ box gelatine or
1 tablespoon granulated gelatine.
¼ cup cold water.
2 cups scalded milk.
Yolks 3 eggs.

⅓ cup sugar.
⅛ teaspoon salt.
1 teaspoon vanilla.
1 tablespoon brandy,
5 lady fingers.

6 macaroons.

Soak gelatine in cold water and add to custard made of milk, eggs, sugar, and salt; strain, cool slightly, and flavor. Place a mould in pan of ice water, decorate with candied cherries and angelica, cover with mixture, added carefully by spoonfuls; when firm, add layer of lady fingers (first soaked in custard), then layer of macaroons (also soaked in custard); repeat, care being taken that each layer is firm before another is added. Garnish, and serve with Cream Sauce I. and candied cherries.

Mont Blanc.

Remove shells from three cups French chestnuts, cook in small quantity of boiling water until soft, when there will be no water remaining. Mash, sweeten to taste with powdered sugar, and moisten with hot milk; cook two minutes. Rub through strainer, cool, flavor with vanilla, Kirsch or Maraschino. Pile in form of pyramid, cover with Cream Sauce I., garnish base with Cream Sauce I. forced through pastry bag and tube.

French Chef.

Crême aux Fruits.

¼ box gelatine or 1 tablespoon granulated gelatine.
¼ cup cold water.
¼ cup scalded milk.
½ cup sugar.

Whites 2 eggs.
½ pint thick cream.
⅓ cup milk.
⅓ cup cooked prunes cut in pieces.

⅓ cup chopped figs.

Soak gelatine in cold water, dissolve in scalded milk, and add sugar. Strain in pan set in ice water, stir constantly, and when it begins to thicken add whites of eggs beaten stiff, cream (diluted with milk and beaten), prunes, and figs. Mould and chill.

To Whip Cream.

Thin and heavy cream are both used in making and garnishing desserts.

Heavy cream is bought in half-pint, pint, and quart glass jars, and usually retails at sixty cents per quart; *thin* or *strawberry cream* comes in glass jars or may be bought in bulk, and usually retails for thirty cents per quart.   Heavy cream is very rich; for which reason, when whipped without being diluted, it is employed as a garnish; even when so used, it is generally diluted with one-fourth to one-third its bulk in milk; when used in

Whipping of cream.

combination with other ingredients for making desserts, it is diluted from one-half to two-thirds its bulk in milk. Thin cream is whipped without being diluted. Cream should be thoroughly chilled for whipping.   Turn cream to be whipped in a bowl (care being taken not to select too large a bowl), and set in pan of crushed ice, to which water is added that cream may be quickly chilled; without addition of water, cream will not be so thoroughly chilled.

For whipping heavy cream undiluted, or diluted with one-third or less its bulk in milk, use Dover egg-beater; undiluted heavy cream if beaten a moment too long will come to butter. Heavy cream diluted, whipped, sweetened, and flavored, is often served with puddings, and called Cream Sauce.

Thin cream is whipped by using a whip churn, as is heavy cream when diluted with one-half to two-thirds its bulk in milk. Place churn in bowl containing cream, hold down cover with left hand, with right hand work dasher with quick downward and slow upward motions; avoid raising dasher too high in cylinder, thus escaping spattering of cream. The first whip which appears should be stirred into cream, as air bubbles are too large and will break; second whip should be removed by spoonfuls to a strainer, strainer to be placed in a pan, as some cream will drain through. The first which drains through may be turned into bowl to be re-whipped, and continue whipping as long as possible.

There will be some cream left in bowl, which does not come above perforations in whip churn, and cannot be whipped. Cream which remains may be scalded and used to dissolve gelatine when making desserts which require gelatine. Cream should treble its bulk in whipping. By following these directions one need have no difficulty, if cream is of right consistency; always bearing in mind heavy cream calls for Dover egg-beater, thin cream for whip churn.

Charlotte Russe.

¼ box gelatine or
1 tablespoon granulated
    gelatine.
¼ cup cold water.
⅓ cup scalded cream.

⅓ cup powdered sugar.
Whip from 3½ cups thin
    cream.
1½ teaspoons vanilla.
6 lady fingers.

Soak gelatine in cold water, dissolve in scalded cream, strain into a bowl, and add sugar and vanilla. Set bowl in pan of ice water and stir constantly until it begins to thicken, then fold in whip from cream, adding one-third at a time. Should gelatine mixture become too thick, melt over hot water, and again cool before adding whip. Trim ends and sides of lady fingers, place around inside of a mould, crust side out, one-half inch apart. Turn in mixture, spread evenly, and chill. Serve on glass dish and garnish with cubes of Wine Jelly. Charlotte Russe is sometimes made in individual moulds; these are often garnished on top with some of mixture forced through a pastry bag and tube. Individual moulds are frequently lined with thin slices of sponge cake cut to fit moulds.

Charlotte Russe garnished with cubes of Wine Jelly.

Orange Trifle.

½ box gelatine or
2 tablespoons granulated
   gelatine.
½ cup cold water.
½ cup boiling water

1 cup sugar.
1 cup orange juice.
Grated rind 1 orange.
1 tablespoon lemon juice.
Whip from 3½ cups cream.

Make same as Charlotte Russe, and mould; or make orange jelly, color with fruit red, and cover bottom of mould one-half inch deep; chill, and when firm fill with Orange Trifle mixture. Cool remaining jelly in shallow pan, cut in cubes, and garnish base of mould.

Banana Cantaloupe.

½ box gelatine or
2 tablespoons granulated gelatine.
½ cup cold water.
Whites 2 eggs.
¼ cup powdered sugar.
¾ cup scalded cream.

⅔ cup sugar.
4 bananas, mashed pulp.
1 tablespoon lemon juice.
Whip from 3½ cups
   cream.
12 lady fingers.

Soak gelatine in cold water, beat whites of eggs slightly, add powdered sugar, and gradually hot cream, cook over hot water until it thickens; add soaked gelatine and remaining sugar, strain into a pan set in ice water, add bananas and lemon juice, stir until it begins to thicken, then fold in whip from cream. Line a melon mould with lady fingers trimmed to just fit sections of mould, turn in the mixture, spread evenly, and chill.

Chocolate Charlotte.

¼ box gelatine or
1 tablespoon granulated gelatine.
¼ cup cold water.
⅓ cup scalded cream.

1½ squares Baker's chocolate.
3 tablespoons hot water.
⅔ cup powdered sugar.
Whip from 3 cups cream.
1 teaspoon vanilla.

6 lady fingers.

Melt chocolate, add half the sugar, dilute with boiling water, and add to gelatine mixture while hot. Proceed same as in recipe for Charlotte Russe.

Caramel Charlotte Russe.

¼ box gelatine or
1 tablespoon granulated gelatine.
¼ cup cold water.
½ cup scalded cream.

⅓ cup sugar caramelized.
¼ cup powdered sugar.
1½ teaspoons vanilla.
Whip from 3½ cups cream.
6 lady fingers.

Make same as Charlotte Russe, adding caramelized sugar to scalded cream before putting into gelatine mixture.

Burnt Almond Charlotte.

½ box gelatine or
2 tablespoons granulated gelatine.
½ cup cold water.
¾ cup scalded milk.
½ cup sugar.

½ cup sugar caramelized.
¾ cup blanched and finely chopped almonds.
1 teaspoon vanilla.
Whip from 3½ cups cream.
6 lady fingers.

Make same as Caramel Charlotte Russe, adding nuts before folding in cream.

Ginger Cream.

¼ box gelatine or
1 tablespoon granulated
   gelatine.
¼ cup cold water.
1 cup milk.
Yolks 2 eggs.
¼ cup sugar.

Few grains salt.
1 tablespoon wine.
½ tablespoon brandy.
2 tablespoons ginger syrup.
¼ cup Canton ginger cut in
   pieces.
Whip from 2½ cups cream.

Soak gelatine, and add to custard made of milk, eggs, sugar, and salt. Strain, chill in pan of ice water, add flavorings, and when it begins to thicken fold in whip from cream.

Orange Charlotte.

⅓ box gelatine or
1⅓ tablespoons granulated
   gelatine.
⅓ cup cold water.
⅓ cup boiling water.

1 cup sugar.
3 tablespoons lemon juice.
1 cup orange juice and pulp.
Whites 3 egg.
Whip from 2 cups cream.

Soak gelatine in cold water, dissolve in boiling water, strain, and add sugar, lemon juice, orange juice, and pulp. Chill in pan of ice water; when quite thick, beat with wire spoon or whisk until frothy, then add whites of eggs beaten stiff, and fold in cream. Line a mould with sections of oranges, turn in mixture, smooth evenly, and chill.

Strawberry Sponge.

⅓ box gelatine or
1⅓ tablespoons granulated
   gelatine.
⅓ cup cold water.
⅓ cup boiling water.

1 cup sugar.
1 tablespoon lemon juice.
1 cup strawberry juice.
Whites 3 eggs.
Whip from 2 cups cream.

Make same as Orange Charlotte.

Orange Baskets.

Cut two pieces from each orange, leaving what remains in shape of basket with handle, remove pulp from baskets and pieces, and keep baskets in ice water until ready to fill. From orange juice make orange jelly with which to fill baskets. Serve garnished with Cream Sauce.

Orange Jelly in Ambush.

Cut oranges in halves lengthwise, remove pulp and juice. With juice make Orange Jelly to fill half the pieces. Fill remaining pieces with Charlotte Russe mixture. When both are firm, put together in pairs and tie together with narrow white ribbon.

Bavarian Cream (Quick).

½ lemon, grated rind and juice.
½ cup white wine.
⅓ cup sugar.

2 eggs.
1 teaspoon granulated gelatine.
1 tablespoon cold water.

Mix lemon, wine, sugar, and yolks of eggs; stir vigorously over fire until mixture thickens, add gelatine soaked in water, then pour over whites of eggs beaten stiff. Set in pan of ice water and beat until thick enough to hold its shape. Turn into a mould lined with lady fingers, and chill. Orange juice may be used in place of wine, and the cream served in orange baskets.

Strawberry Bavarian Cream.

Line a mould with large, fresh strawberries cut in halves, fill with Charlotte Russe mixture.

Pineapple Bavarian Cream.

½ box gelatine or
2 tablespoons granulated gelatine.
½ cup cold water.

1 can grated pineapple.
½ cup sugar.
1 tablespoon lemon juice.
Whip from 3 cups cream.

Soak gelatine in cold water. Heat pineapple, add sugar, lemon juice, and soaked gelatine; chill in pan of ice water, stirring constantly; when it begins to thicken, fold in whip from cream, mould, and chill.

Royal Diplomatic Pudding.

Place mould in pan of ice water and pour in Wine Jelly II. one-half inch deep. When firm, decorate with candied cherries and angelica, proceed as for Fruit Chartreuse, filling the centre with Charlotte Russe mixture or Fruit Cream.

Fruit Cream.

Peel four bananas, mash, and rub through a sieve; add pulp and juice of two oranges, one tablespoon lemon juice, one tablespoon sherry wine, two-thirds cup powdered sugar, and one and one-fourth tablespoons granulated gelatine dissolved in one-fourth cup boiling water. Cool in ice water, stirring constantly, and fold in whip from two cups cream.

CHAPTER V.

ICES, ICE CREAMS, AND OTHER FROZEN DESSERTS.

ICES and other frozen dishes comprise the most popular desserts. Hygienically speaking, they cannot be recommended for the final course of a dinner, as cold mixtures reduce the temperature of the stomach, thus retarding digestion until the normal temperature is again reached. But how cooling, refreshing, and nourishing, when properly taken, and of what inestimable value in the sick room!

Frozen dishes include : —

Water Ice, — fruit juice sweetened, diluted with water, and frozen.

Sherbet, — water ice to which is added a small quantity of dissolved gelatine or beaten whites of eggs.

Frappé, — water ice frozen to consistency of mush; in freezing, equal parts of salt and ice being used to make it granular.

Punch, — water ice to which is added spirit and spice.

Sorbet, — strictly speaking, frozen punch; the name is often given to a water ice where several kinds of fruit are used.

Philadelphia Ice Cream, — thin cream, sweetened, flavored, and frozen.

Plain Ice Cream, — custard foundation, thin cream, and flavoring.

Mousse, — heavy cream, beaten until stiff, sweetened, flavored, placed in a mould, packed in equal parts salt and ice, and allowed to stand three hours; or whip from thin cream may be used folded into mixture containing small quantity of gelatine.

How to Freeze Desserts.

The prejudice of thinking a frozen dessert difficult to prepare has long since been overcome. With ice cream freezer, burlap bag, wooden mallet or axe, small saucepan, sufficient ice and coarse rock salt, the process neither takes much time nor patience. Snow may be used instead of ice; if not readily acted on by salt, pour in one cup cold water. Crush ice finely by placing in bag and giving a few blows with mallet or broad side of axe; if there are any coarse pieces, remove them. Place can containing mixture to be frozen in wooden tub, cover, and adjust top. Turn crank to make sure can fits in socket. Allow three level measures ice to one of salt, and repeat until ice and salt come to top of can, packing solidly, using handle of mallet to force it down. If only small quantity is to be frozen, the ice and salt need come only little higher in the tub than mixture to be frozen. These are found the best proportions of ice and salt to insure smooth, fine-grained cream, sherbet, or water ice, while equal parts of salt and ice are used for freezing frappé. If a larger proportion of salt is used, mixture will freeze in shorter time and be of granular consistency, which is desirable only for frappé.

The mixture increases in bulk during freezing, so the can should never be more than three-fourths filled; by overcrowding can, cream will be made coarse grained. Turn the crank slowly and steadily to expose as large surface of mixture as possible to ice and salt. After frozen to a mush, the crank may be turned more rapidly, adding more ice and salt if needed; never draw off salt water until mixture is frozen, unless there is possibility of its getting into the can, for salt water is what effects freezing; until ice melts, no change will take place. After freezing is accomplished, draw off water, remove dasher, and with spoon pack solidly. Put cork in opening of cover, then put on cover. Re-pack freezer, using four measures ice to one of salt. Place over top newspapers or piece of carpet; when serving time comes, remove can, wipe carefully, and place in vessel of cool water; let stand one minute, remove cover, and run a knife around edge of cream, invert can on serving-dish, and frozen mixture will slip out. Should there be any difficulty, a cloth wrung out of hot water, passed over can, will aid in removing mixture.

To Line a Mould.

Allow mould to stand in salt and ice until well chilled. Remove cover, put in mixture by spoonfuls, and spread with back of spoon or a case knife evenly three-quarters inch thick.

To Mould Frozen Mixtures.

When frozen mixtures are to be bricked or moulded, avoid freezing too hard. Pack mixture solidly in moulds and cover with buttered paper, buttered side up. Have moulds so well filled that mixture is forced down sides of mould when cover is pressed down. Repack in salt and ice, using four parts ice to one part salt. If these directions are carefully followed, one may feel no fear that salt water will enter cream, even though moulds be immersed in salt water.

Lemon Ice.

4 cups water.   2 cups sugar.
¾ cup lemon juice.

Make a syrup by boiling water and sugar twenty minutes; add lemon juice; cool, strain, and freeze. See directions for freezing, page 75.

Orange Ice.

4 cups water.   ¼ cup lemon juice.
2 cups sugar.   Grated rind of two
2 cups orange juice.   oranges.

Make syrup as for Lemon Ice; add fruit juice and grated rind; cool, strain, and freeze.

Pomegranate Ice.

Same as Orange Ice, made from blood oranges.

Raspberry Ice.

4 cups water.	2 cups raspberry juice.
1⅔ cups sugar.	2 tablespoons lemon juice.

Make a syrup as for Lemon Ice, cool, add raspberries mashed, and squeezed through double cheese cloth, and lemon juice; strain and freeze.

Strawberry Ice.

4 cups water.	2 cups strawberry juice.
1½ cups sugar.	1 tablespoon lemon juice.

Prepare and freeze same as Raspberry Ice.

Currant Ice.

4 cups water.	1½ cups sugar.
2 cups currant juice.	

Prepare and freeze same as Raspberry Ice.

Raspberry and Currant Ice.

4 cups water.	⅔ cup raspberry juice.
1⅓ cups sugar.	1⅓ cups currant juice.

Prepare and freeze same as Raspberry Ice.

Crême de Menthe Ice.

4 cups water.	⅓ cup Crême de Menthe cordial.
1 cup sugar.	Burnett's Leaf Green.

Make a syrup as for Lemon Ice, add cordial and coloring; strain and freeze.

Canton Sherbet.

4 cups water.	¼ lb. Canton ginger.
1 cup sugar.	½ cup orange juice.
⅓ cup lemon juice.	

Cut ginger in small pieces, add water and sugar, boil fifteen minutes; add fruit juice, cool, strain, and freeze. To be used in place of punch at a course dinner. This quantity is enough to serve twelve persons.

Milk Sherbet.

4 cups milk.	1½ cups sugar.
Juice 3 lemons.	

Mix juice and sugar, stirring constantly while slowly adding milk; if added too rapidly mixture will have a curdled appearance, which is unsightly, but will not affect the quality of sherbet; freeze and serve.

Pineapple Frappé.

2 cups water.	2 cups ice water.
1 cup sugar.	1 can grated pineapple or
Juice 3 lemons.	1 pineapple shredded.

Make a syrup by boiling water and sugar fifteen minutes; add pineapple and lemon juice; cool, strain, add ice water, and freeze to a mush, using equal parts ice and salt. Serve in frappé glasses. If fresh fruit is used, more sugar will be required.

Sorbet.

2 cups water.	1⅓ cups orange juice.
2 cups sugar.	½ cup lemon juice.
1 can grated pineapple or	1 quart Apollinaris.
1 pineapple shredded.	

Prepare and freeze same as Pineapple Frappé.

Café Frappé.

White 1 egg.	½ cup ground coffee.
½ cup cold water.	4 cups boiling water.
	1 cup sugar.

Beat white of egg slightly, add cold water, and mix with coffee; turn into scalded coffee-pot, add boiling water, and boil one minute; place on back of range ten minutes; strain, add sugar, cool, and freeze as Pineapple Frappé. Serve in frappé glasses, with whipped cream, sweetened and flavored.

Clam Frappé.

20 clams.	½ cup cold water.

Wash clams thoroughly, changing water several times; put in stewpan with cold water, cover closely, and steam until shells open. Strain the liquor, cool, and freeze to a mush.

Frozen Apricots.

1 can apricots.	1½ cups sugar.
	Water.

Drain apricots, and cut in small pieces. To the syrup add enough water to make four cups, and cook with sugar five minutes; strain, add apricots, cool, and freeze. Peaches may be used instead of apricots. To make a richer dessert, add the whip from two cups cream when frozen to a mush, and continue freezing.

Pineapple Cream.

2 cups water.	1 can grated pineapple.
1 cup sugar.	2 cups cream.

Make syrup by boiling sugar and water fifteen minutes; strain, cool, add pineapple, and freeze to a mush. Fold in whip from cream; let stand thirty minutes before serving.

Cardinal Punch.

4 cups water.	⅓ cup lemon juice.
2 cups sugar.	¼ cup brandy.
⅔ cup orange juice.	¼ cup Curaçoa.
¼ cup tea infusion.	

Make syrup as for Lemon Ice, add fruit juice and tea, freeze to a mush; add strong liquors and continue freezing. Serve in frappé glasses.

Punch Hollandaise.

4 cups water.	Rind one lemon.
1⅓ cups sugar.	1 can grated pineapple.
⅓ cup lemon juice.	¼ cup brandy.
2 tablespoons gin.	

Cook sugar, water, and lemon rind fifteen minutes, add lemon juice and pineapple, cool, strain, freeze to a mush, add strong liquors, and continue freezing.

Victoria Punch.

3½ cups water.	Grated rind two oranges.
2 cups sugar.	1 cup angelica wine.
½ cup lemon juice.	1 cup cider.
½ cup orange juice.	1½ tablespoons gin.

Prepare same as Cardinal Punch; strain before freezing, to remove orange rind.

London Sherbet.

2 cups sugar.	3 tablespoons lemon juice.
2 cups water.	1 cup fruit syrup.
⅓ cup seeded and finely cut raisins.	¼ grated nutmeg.
	¼ cup port wine.
¾ cup orange juice.	Whites 3 eggs.

Make syrup by boiling water and sugar ten minutes; pour over raisins, cool, and add fruit syrup and nutmeg; freeze to a mush, then add wine and whites of eggs beaten stiff, and continue freezing. Serve in glasses. Fruit syrup may be used which has been left from canned peaches, pears, or strawberries.

Roman Punch.

4 cups water.	½ cup orange juice.
2 cups sugar.	½ cup tea infusion.
½ cup lemon juice.	½ cup rum.

Prepare and freeze same as Cardinal Punch.

Vanilla Ice Cream I. (Philadelphia).

1 quart thin cream.	¾ cup sugar.

1½ tablespoons vanilla.

Mix ingredients, and freeze.

Vanilla Ice Cream II.

2 cups scalded milk.	1 egg.
1 tablespoon flour.	⅛ teaspoon salt.
1 cup sugar.	1 quart thin cream.

2 tablespoons vanilla.

Mix flour, sugar, and salt, add egg slightly beaten, and milk gradually; cook over hot water twenty minutes, stirring constantly at first; should custard have curdled appearance, it will disappear in freezing. When cool, add cream and flavoring; strain and freeze.

Vanilla Ice Cream Croquettes.

Shape Vanilla Ice Cream in individual moulds, roll in macaroon dust made by pounding and sifting dry macaroons.

Chocolate Ice Cream I.

1 quart thin cream.	1½ squares Baker's chocolate or
1 cup sugar.	¼ cup prepared cocoa.
Few grains salt.	1 tablespoon vanilla.

Melt chocolate and dilute with hot water to pour easily, add to cream; then add sugar, salt, and flavoring, and freeze.

Chocolate Ice Cream II.

Use recipe for Vanilla Ice Cream II. Melt two squares Baker's chocolate, and pour hot custard slowly on chocolate; then cool before adding cream.

Strawberry Ice Cream.

3 pints thin cream.	1¾ cups sugar.
2 boxes strawberries.	2 cups milk.

1½ tablespoons arrowroot.

Wash and hull berries, sprinkle with sugar, let stand one hour, mash, and rub through strainer. Scald one and one-half cups milk; dilute arrowroot with remaining milk, add to hot milk, and cook ten minutes in double boiler; cool, add cream, freeze to a mush, add fruit, and finish freezing.

Pineapple Ice Cream

3 pints cream.	½ cup sugar.

1 can grated pineapple.

Add pineapple to cream, let stand thirty minutes; strain, add sugar, and freeze.

Coffee Ice Cream.

1 quart cream.	1¼ cups sugar.
1½ cups milk.	¼ teaspoon salt.
⅓ cup Mocha coffee.	Yolks 4 eggs.

Scald milk with coffee, add one cup sugar; mix egg yolks slightly beaten with one-fourth cup sugar, and salt; combine mixtures, cook over hot water until thickened, add one cup cream, and let stand on back of range twenty-five minutes; cool, add remaining cream, and strain through double cheese cloth; freeze. Coffee Ice Cream may be served with Maraschino cherries.

Caramel Ice Cream.

1 quart cream.	1 egg.
2 cups milk.	1 tablespoon flour.
1⅓ cups sugar.	⅛ teaspoon salt.
	1½ tablespoons vanilla.

Prepare same as Vanilla Ice Cream II., using one-half sugar in custard; remaining half caramelize, and add slowly to hot custard.

Burnt Almond Ice Cream.

It is made same as Caramel Ice Cream, with the addition of one cup finely chopped blanched almonds.

Brown Bread Ice Cream.

3 pints cream.	⅞ cup sugar.
1¼ cups dried brown bread crumbs.	¼ teaspoon salt.

Soak crumbs in one quart cream, let stand fifteen minutes, rub through sieve, add sugar, salt, and remaining cream; then freeze.

Bisque Ice Cream.

Make custard as for Vanilla Ice Cream II., add one quart cream, one tablespoon vanilla, and one cup hickory nut or English walnut meat finely chopped.

Macaroon Ice Cream.

1 quart cream.	¾ cup sugar.
1 cup macaroons.	1 tablespoon vanilla.

Dry, pound, and measure macaroons; add to cream, sugar, and vanilla, then freeze.

Banana Ice Cream.

1 quart cream.	1½ tablespoons lemon juice.
4 bananas.	1 cup sugar.

Remove skins, and rub bananas through a sieve; add remaining ingredients; then freeze.

Ginger Ice Cream.

To recipe for Vanilla Ice Cream II., using one-half quantity vanilla, add one-half cup Canton ginger cut in small pieces, three tablespoons ginger syrup, and two tablespoons wine; then freeze.

Pistachio Ice Cream.

Prepare as Vanilla Ice Cream II., using for flavoring one tablespoon vanilla and one teaspoon almond extract; color with Burnett's Leaf Green.

Pistachio Bisque.

To Pistachio Ice Cream add one-half cup each of pounded macaroons, chopped almonds and peanuts. Mould, and serve with or without Claret Sauce.

Neapolitan or Harlequin Ice Cream.

Two kinds of ice cream and an ice moulded in a brick.

Baked Alaska.

Whites 6 eggs.	2 quart brick of ice cream.
6 tablespoons powdered sugar.	Thin sheet sponge cake.

Make meringue of eggs and sugar as in Meringue I., cover a board with white paper, lay on sponge cake, turn ice cream on cake (which should extend one-half inch beyond cream), cover with meringue, and spread smoothly. Place on oven grate and brown quickly in hot oven.

The board, paper, cake, and méringue are poor conductors of heat, and prevent the cream from melting. Slip from paper on ice cream platter.

Pudding Glacé.

2 cups milk.	¼ teaspoon salt.
⅔ cup raisins.	1 quart thin cream.
1 cup sugar.	½ cup almonds.
1 egg.	½ cup candied pineapple.
1 tablespoon flour.	⅓ cup Canton ginger.

3 tablespoons wine.

Scald raisins in milk fifteen minutes, strain, make custard of milk, egg, sugar, flour, and salt; strain, cool, add pineapple, ginger cut in small pieces, nuts finely chopped, wine, and cream; then freeze. The raisins should be rinsed and saved for a pudding.

Frozen Pudding I.

2½ cups milk.	2 eggs.
1 cup sugar.	1 cup heavy cream.
⅛ teaspoonful salt.	¼ cup rum.

1 cup candied fruit, cherries, pineapples, pears, and apricots.

Cut fruit in pieces, and soak several hours in brandy to cover, which prevents fruit freezing; make custard of first four ingredients; strain, cool, add cream and rum, then freeze. Fill a brick mould with alternate layers of the cream and fruit; pack in salt and ice and let stand two hours.

Frozen Pudding II.

1 quart cream.	¼ cup rum.
¾ cup sugar.	1 cup candied fruit.

8 lady fingers.

Cut fruit in pieces, and soak several hours in brandy to cover. Mix cream, sugar, and rum, then freeze. Line a two quart melon mould with lady fingers, crust side down; fill with alternate layers of the cream and fruit, cover, pack in salt and ice, and let stand two hours. Brandied peaches cut in pieces, with some of their syrup added, greatly improve the pudding.

Frozen Pudding.

Delmonico Ice Cream with Angel Food.

2 cups milk.	⅛ teaspoon salt.
¾ cup sugar.	2½ cups thin cream.
Yolks 7 eggs.	1 tablespoon vanilla.

1 teaspoon lemon.

Make custard of milk, sugar, eggs, and salt; cool, strain, and flavor; whip cream, remove whip; there should be two quarts; add to custard, and freeze. Serve plain or with Angel Food.

Angel Food.

Whites 3 eggs.	1 quart cream whip.
½ cup powdered sugar.	1½ teaspoons vanilla.

Beat eggs until stiff, fold in sugar, cream whip, and flavoring; line a mould with Delmonico Ice Cream, fill with the mixture, cover, pack in salt and ice, and let stand two hours.

Sultana Roll with Claret Sauce.

Line one-pound baking-powder boxes with Pistachio Ice Cream; sprinkle with sultana raisins which have

been soaked one hour in brandy; fill centres with Vanilla
Ice Cream or whipped cream, sweetened, and flavored with
vanilla; cover with Pistachio Ice Cream; pack in salt and
ice, and let stand one and one-half hours.

Claret Sauce.

1 cup sugar.   ¼ cup water.
            ⅓ cup claret.

Boil sugar and water eight minutes; cool slightly, and
add claret.

Café Parfait.

1 cup milk.   ⅛ teaspoon salt.
¼ cup Mocha coffee.   1 cup sugar.
Yolks 3 eggs.   3 cups thin cream.

Scald milk with coffee, and add one-half the sugar;
without straining, use this mixture for making custard,
with eggs, salt, and remaining sugar; add one cup cream
and let stand thirty minutes; cool, strain through double
cheese cloth, add remaining cream, and freeze. Line a
mould, fill with Italian Meringue, cover, pack in salt and
ice, and let stand three hours.

Italian Meringue.

½ cup sugar.   Whites 3 eggs.
¼ cup water.   1 cup thin cream.
1 tablespoon gelatine or   ½ tablespoon vanilla.
¼ teaspoon granulated gelatine.

Make syrup by boiling sugar and water; pour slowly on
beaten whites of eggs, and continue beating. Place in
pan of ice water, and beat until cold; dissolve gelatine
in small quantity boiling water; strain into mixture; whip
cream, fold in whip, and flavor.

Bombe Glacée.

Line a mould with sherbet or water ice; fill with ice
cream or thin Charlotte Russe mixture; cover, pack in

salt and ice, and let stand two hours. The mould may be lined with ice cream. Pomegranate Ice and Vanilla or Macaroon Ice Cream make a good combination.

Nesselrode Pudding.

3 cups milk.	½ teaspoon salt.
1½ cups sugar.	1 pint thin cream.
Yolks 5 eggs.	¼ cup pineapple syrup.

1½ cups prepared French chestnuts.

Make custard of first four ingredients, strain, cool; add cream, pineapple syrup, and chestnuts; then freeze. To prepare chestnuts, shell, cook in boiling water until soft, and force through a strainer. Line a two-quart melon mould with part of mixture; to remainder add one-half cup candied fruit cut in small pieces, one-quarter cup sultana raisins, and eight chestnuts broken in pieces, first soaked several hours in Maraschino syrup. Fill mould, cover, pack in salt and ice, and let stand two hours. Serve with whipped cream, sweetened and flavored with Maraschino syrup.

Strawberry Mousse.

1 quart thin cream.	¼ box gelatine (scant) or
1 box strawberries.	1¼ tablespoons granulated gelatine.
1 cup sugar	2 tablespoons cold water.

3 tablespoons hot water.

Wash and hull berries, sprinkle with sugar, and let stand one hour; mash, and rub through a fine sieve; add gelatine soaked in cold and dissolved in boiling water. Set in pan of ice water and stir until it begins to thicken; then fold in whip from cream, put in mould, cover, pack in salt and ice, and let stand four hours. Raspberries may be used in place of strawberries.

Coffee Mousse.

Make same as Strawberry Mousse, using one cup boiled coffee in place of fruit juice.

Mousse Marron.

1 quart vanilla ice cream.	1 teaspoon granulated gelatine.
½ cup sugar.	1½ cups prepared French chestnuts.
¼ cup water.	1 pint cream.
Whites two eggs.	½ tablespoon vanilla.

Cook sugar and water five minutes, pour on to beaten whites of eggs; dissolve gelatine in one and one-half tablespoons boiling water, and add to first mixture. Set in a pan of ice water, and stir until cold; add chestnuts, and fold in whip from cream and vanilla. Line a mould with ice cream, and fill with mixture; cover, pack in salt and ice, and let stand three hours.

Cardinal Mousse, with Iced Madeira Sauce.

Line a mould with Pomegranate Ice; fill with Italian Meringue made of three-fourths cup sugar, one-third cup hot water, whites two eggs, and one and one-half teaspoons granulated gelatine dissolved in two tablespoons boiling water. Beat until cold, and fold in whip from two cups cream; flavor with one teaspoon vanilla, cover, pack in salt and ice, and let stand three hours.

Iced Madeira Sauce.

¼ cup orange juice.	½ cup sugar.
2 tablespoons lemon juice.	1 cup boiling water.
½ cup Madeira wine.	Whites 2 eggs.

Freeze fruit juice and wine; boil sugar and water, pour on slowly to beaten whites of eggs, set in a pan of salted ice water, and stir until cold   Add to frozen mixture.

Demi-glacé aux Fraises.

Line a brick mould with Vanilla Ice Cream, put in layer of Lady Fingers, and fill the centre with preserved strawberries or large fresh fruit cut in halves; cover with ice cream, pack in salt and ice, and let stand one hour. For ice cream, make custard of two and one-half cups milk, yolks four eggs, one cup sugar, and one-fourth teaspoon salt; strain, cool, add one cup heavy cream and one tablespoon vanilla; then freeze.

CHAPTER VI.

PASTRY.

PASTRY cannot be easily excluded from the menu of the New Englander. Who can dream of a Thanksgiving dinner without a pie! The last decade has done much to remove pies from the *daily* bill of fare, and in their place are found delicate puddings and seasonable fruits.

If pastry is to be served, have it of the best, — light, flaky, and tender.

To pastry belongs, 1st, Puff Paste; 2d, Plain Paste.

Puff paste, which to many seems so difficult of preparation, is rarely attempted by any except professionals. As a matter of fact, one who has never handled a rolling pin is less liable to fail, under the guidance of a good teacher, than an old cook, who finds it difficult to overcome the bad habit of using too much force in rolling. It is necessary to work rapidly and with a light touch. A cold room is of great advantage.

For making pastry, pastry flour and the best shortenings, thoroughly chilled, are essential. Its lightness depends on the amount of air enclosed and expansion of that air in baking. The flakiness depends upon kind and amount of shortening used. Lard makes more tender crust than butter, but lacks flavor which butter gives. Puff paste is usually shortened with butter, though some chefs prefer beef suet. Eggs and ice were formerly used, but are not essentials.

Butter should be washed if pastry is to be of the best, so as to remove salt and buttermilk, thus making it of a waxy consistency, easy to handle.

Rules for Washing Butter. Scald and chill an earthen bowl. Heat palms of hands in hot water, and chill in cold water. By following these directions, butter will not adhere to bowl nor hands. Wash butter in bowl by squeezing with hands until soft and waxy, placing bowl under a cold-water faucet and allowing water to run. A small amount of butter may be washed by using a wooden spoon in place of the hands.

For rolling paste, use a smooth wooden board, and wooden rolling-pin with handles.

Puff paste should be used for vol-au-vents, patties, rissoles, bouchées, cheese straws, tarts, etc. It may be used for rims and upper crusts of pies, but never for lower crusts. Plain paste may be used where pastry is needed, except for vol-au-vents and patties.

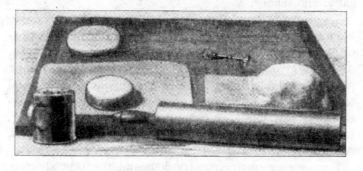

Puff paste before and after folding in butter.

Puff Paste.

1 pound butter.   1 pound pastry flour.
                    Cold water.

Wash the butter, pat and fold until no water flies. Reserve two tablespoons of butter, and shape remainder into a circular piece one-half inch thick, and put on floured board. Work two tablespoons of butter into flour with the tips of fingers of the right hand. Moisten to a dough with cold water, turn on slightly floured board, and knead one minute. Cover with towel, and let stand five minutes.

Pat and roll one-fourth inch thick, keeping paste a little wider than long, and corners square. If this cannot be accomplished with rolling-pin, draw into shape with fingers. Place butter on centre of lower half of paste. Cover butter by folding upper half of paste over it. Press edges firmly to enclose as much air as possible.

Fold right side of paste over enclosed butter, the left side under enclosed butter. Turn paste half-way round, cover, and let stand five minutes. Pat and roll one-fourth inch thick, having paste longer than wide, lifting often to prevent paste from sticking, and dredging board slightly with flour when necessary. Fold from ends towards centre, making three layers. Cover, and let stand five minutes. Repeat twice, turning paste half-way round each time before rolling. After fourth rolling, fold from ends to centre, and double, making four layers. Put in cold place to chill; if outside temperature is not sufficiently cold, fold paste in a towel, put in a dripping-pan, and place between dripping pans of crushed ice. If paste is to be kept for several days, wrap in a napkin, put in tin pail and cover tightly, then put in cold place; if in ice box, do not allow pail to come in direct contact with ice.

To Bake Puff Paste.

Baking of puff paste requires as much care and judgment as making. After shaping, chill thoroughly before baking. Puff paste requires hot oven, greatest heat coming from the bottom, that the paste may properly rise. While rising it is often necessary to decrease the heat by lifting covers or opening the check to stove. Turn frequently that it may rise evenly. When it has risen its full height, slip a pan under the sheet on which paste is baking to prevent burning on the bottom. Puff paste should be baked on a tin sheet covered with a double thickness of brown paper, or dripping-pan may be used, lined with brown paper. The temperature for baking of patties should be about the same as for raised biscuit; vol-au-vents require less heat, and are covered for first half-hour to prevent scorching on top.

Patty Shells.

Roll puff paste one-quarter inch thick, shape with a patty cutter, first dipped in flour; remove centres from one-half the rounds with smaller cutter. Brush over with cold water the larger pieces near the edge, and fit on rings, pressing lightly. Place in towel between pans of crushed ice, and chill until paste is stiff; if cold weather, chill out of doors. Place on iron or tin sheet covered with brown paper, and bake twenty-five minutes in hot oven. The shells should rise their full height and begin to brown in twelve to fifteen minutes; continue browning, and finish baking in twenty-five minutes. Pieces cut from centre of rings of patties may be baked and used for patty covers, or put together, rolled, and cut for unders. Trimmings from puff paste should be carefully laid on top of each other, patted, and rolled out.

Vol-au-vents.

Roll puff paste one-third inch thick, mark an oval on paste with cutter or mould, and cut out with sharp knife, first dipped in flour. Brush over near the edge with cold water, put on a rim three-fourths inch wide, press lightly, chill, and bake. Vol-au-vents require for baking forty-five minutes to one hour. During the first half-hour they should be covered, watched carefully, and frequently turned. The paste cut from centre of rim should be rolled one-quarter inch thick, shaped same size as before rolling, chilled, baked, and used for cover to the Vol-au-vent.

Plain Paste.

1½ cups flour.   ¼ cup butter.
¼ cup lard.   ½ teaspoon salt.
                Cold water.

Wash butter, pat, and form in circular piece.   Add salt
to flour, and work in lard with tips of fingers or case knife.
Moisten to dough with cold water; ice water is not an
essential, but is desirable in summer.   Toss on board
dredged sparingly with flour, pat, and roll out; fold in
butter as for puff paste, pat, and roll out.   Fold so as to
make three layers, turn half-way round, pat, and roll out;
repeat.   The pastry may be used at once; if not, fold in
cheese cloth, put in covered tin, and keep in cold place,
but never in direct contact with ice.   Plain paste requires
a moderate oven.   This is superior paste and quickly
made.

Quick Paste.

1½ cups flour.   ¼ cup cottolene or cocoanut
¾ teaspoon salt.   butter.
                Cold water.

Mix salt with flour, cut in shortening with knife.   Moisten
to dough with cold water.   Toss on floured board, pat,
roll out, and roll up like a jelly roll.   Use one-third cup of
shortening if a richer paste is desired.

Paste with Lard.

1½ cups flour.   ⅓ cup lard.
½ teaspoon salt.   Cold water.

Mix salt with flour.   Reserve one and one-fourth tablespoons lard, work in remainder to flour, using tips of fingers or a case knife.   Moisten to a dough with water.
Toss on a floured board, pat, and roll out.   Spread with
one tablespoon reserved lard, dredge with flour, roll up
like a jelly roll, pat, and roll out; again roll up.   Cut
from the end of roll a piece large enough to line a pie plate.
Pat and roll out, keeping the paste as circular in form as

possible. With care and experience there need be no trimmings. Worked-over pastry is never as satisfactory. The remaining one-fourth tablespoon lard is used to dot over upper crust of pie just before sending to oven; this gives the pie a flaky appearance. Ice water has a similar effect. If milk is brushed over the pie it has a glazed appearance. This quantity of paste will make one pie with two crusts and a few puffs, or two pies with one crust where the rim is built up and fluted.

Pop-overs
(page 33)

Orange Ice
(page 76)

Banana Cake
(page 153)

Brownies
(page 149)

Tapioca Custard Pudding
(page 43)

Bread Pudding
(page 44)

Cocoanut Cake
(page 169)

Jelly Roll
(page 144)

Crescents
(page 168)

Lemon Pie
(page 116)

Apple Pie
(page 114)

Oatmeal Cookies
(page 131)

Pound Cake
(page 156)

Baked Custard
(page 56)

Pineapple
Ice Cream
(page 82)

Lemon Soufflé
(page 47)

CHAPTER VII.

PIES.

PASTE for pies should be one-fourth inch thick and rolled a little larger than the plate to allow for shrinking. In dividing paste for pies, allow more for upper than under crusts. Always perforate upper crusts that steam may escape. Some make a design, others pierce with a large fork.

Flat rims for pies should be cut in strips three-fourths inch wide. Under crusts should be brushed with cold water before putting on rims, and rims slightly fulled, otherwise they will shrink from edge of plate. The pastry-jagger, a simple device for cutting paste, makes rims with fluted edges.

Pies requiring two crusts sometimes have a rim between the crusts. This is mostly confined to mince pies, where there is little danger of juice escaping. Sometimes a rim is placed over upper crust. Where two pieces of paste are put together, the under piece should always be brushed with cold water, the upper piece placed over, and the two pressed lightly together; otherwise they will separate during baking.

When juicy fruit is used for filling pies, some of the juices are apt to escape during baking. As a precaution, bind with a strip of cotton cloth wrung out of cold water and cut one inch wide and long enough to encircle the plate. Squash, pumpkin, and custard pies are much less care during baking when bound. Where cooked fruits are used for filling, it is desirable to bake crusts separately. This is best accomplished by covering an inverted deep

pie plate with paste and baking for under crust. Prick
with a fork before baking. Slip from plate and fill. For
upper crusts, roll a piece of paste a little larger than the
pie plate, prick, and bake on a tin sheet.

For baking pies, perforated tin plates are used. They
may be bought shallow or deep. By the use of such plates
the under crust is well cooked. Pastry should be thoroughly baked and well browned. Pies require from thirty-
five to forty-five minutes for baking. Never grease a pie
plate; good pastry greases its own tin. Slip pies, when
slightly cooled, to earthen plates.

Apple Pie I.

4 or 5 sour apples.	⅛ teaspoon salt.
⅓ cup sugar.	1 teaspoon butter.
¼ teaspoon grated nutmeg.	1 teaspoon lemon juice.

Few gratings lemon rind.

Line pie plate with paste. Pare, core, and cut the
apples into eighths, put row around plate one-half inch
from edge, and work towards centre until plate is covered;
then pile on remainder. Mix sugar, nutmeg, salt, lemon
juice, and grated rind, and sprinkle over apples. Dot
over with butter. Wet edges of under crust, cover with
upper crust, and press edges together.

Bake forty to forty-five minutes in moderate oven. A
very good pie may be made without butter, lemon juice
and grated rind. Cinnamon may be substituted for nutmeg. Evaporated apples may be used in place of fresh
fruit. If used, they should be soaked over night in cold
water.

Apple Pie II.

Use same ingredients as for Apple Pie I. Place in
small earthen baking-dish and add hot water to prevent
apples from burning. Cover closely and bake three hours
in very slow oven, when apples will be a dark red color.
Brown sugar may be used instead of white sugar, a little
more being required. Cool, and bake between two crusts.

Blackberry Pie.

Pick over and wash one and one-half cups berries. Stew until soft with enough water to prevent burning. Add sugar to taste and one-eighth teaspoon salt. Line plate with paste, put on a rim, fill with berries (which have been cooled); arrange six strips pastry across the top, cut same width as rim; put on an upper rim. Bake thirty minutes in moderate oven.

Blueberry Pie.

2½ cups berries.	½ cup supar.
Flour.	⅛ teaspoon salt.

Line a deep plate with Plain Paste, fill with berries slightly dredged with flour; sprinkle with sugar and salt, cover, and bake forty-five to fifty minutes in a moderate oven. For sweetening, some prefer to use one-third molasses, the remaining two-thirds to be sugar. Six green grapes (from which seeds have been removed) cut in small pieces much improve the flavor, particularly where huckleberries are used in place of blueberries.

Cranberry Pie.

1½ cups cranberries.	½ cup water.
¾ cup sugar.	

Put ingredients in saucepan in order given, and cook ten minutes; cool, and bake in one crust, with a rim, and strips across the top.

Currant Pie.

1 cup currants.	¼ cup flour.
1 cup sugar.	2 egg yolks.
2 tablespoons water.	

Mix flour and sugar, add yolks of eggs slightly beaten and diluted with water. Wash currants, drain, remove stems, then measure; add to first mixture and bake in one crust; cool, and cover with Meringue I. Cook in slow oven until delicately browned.

Cream Pie.

Bake three crusts on separate pie plates. Put together with Cream Filling and dust over with powdered sugar. If allowed to stand after filling for any length of time, the pastry will soften.

Custard Pie.

2 eggs.	⅛ teaspoon salt.
3 tablespoons sugar.	1½ cups milk.

Few gratings nutmeg.

Beat eggs slightly, add sugar, salt, and milk. Line plate with paste, and build up a fluted rim. Strain in the mixture and sprinkle with few gratings nutmeg. Bake in quick oven at first to set rim, decrease the heat afterwards, as egg and milk in combination need to be cooked at low temperature.

Date Pie.

2 cups milk.	2 eggs.
⅓ pound sugar dates.	¼ teaspoon salt.

Few gratings nutmeg.

Cook dates with milk twenty minutes in top of double boiler. Strain and rub through sieve, then add eggs and salt. Bake same as Custard Pie.

Lemon Pie I.

½ cup chopped apple.	¼ cup rolled common crackers.
1 cup sugar.	2 tablespoons lemon juice.
1 beaten egg.	Grated rind 1 lemon.

1 teaspoon melted butter.

Mix ingredients in order given and bake with two crusts.

Lemon Pie II.

¾ cup sugar.	2 egg yolks.
¾ cup boiling water.	3 tablespoons lemon juice.
3 tablespoons corn-starch.	Grated rind 1 lemon.

1 teaspoon butter.

Mix corn-starch and sugar, add boiling water, stirring constantly. Cook two minutes, add butter, egg yolks,

and rind and juice of lemon.   Line plate with paste same
as for Custard Pie.   Turn in mixture which has been
cooled, and bake until pastry is well browned.   Cool
slightly and cover with Meringue I.; then return to oven
and bake meringue.

Lemon Pie III.

Yolks 4 eggs.	Whites 4 eggs.
6 tablespoons sugar.	1¼ cups milk.
Few grains salt.	1 cup powdered sugar.

1 lemon.

Beat yolks of eggs slightly, add sugar, salt, grated rind
of lemon, and milk.   Line plate with paste as for Custard
Pie.   Pour in mixture.   Bake in moderate oven until set.
Remove, cool slightly, and cover with Meringue III. made
of whites of eggs, powdered sugar, and lemon juice.

Lemon Pie IV.

Lemon Pie IV.

3 eggs.	¼ cup lemon juice.
⅔ cup sugar.	Grated rind ½ lemon.

2 tablespoons water.

Beat eggs slightly, add sugar, lemon juice, grated rind,
and water.   Bake in one crust.   Cool slightly, cover with
Meringue II., then return to oven and bake meringue.

Mince Pies.

Mince pies should be always baked with two crusts. For Thanksgiving and Christmas pies, Puff Paste is often used for rims and upper crusts.

Mince Pie Meat.

4 lbs. lean beef.	3 lbs. currants.
2 lbs. beef suet.	½ lb. finely cut citron.
Baldwin apples.	1 quart cooking brandy.
3 quinces.	1 tablespoon cinnamon and mace.
3 lbs. sugar.	1 tablespoon powdered clove.
2 cups molasses.	2 grated nutmegs.
2 quarts cider.	1 teaspoon pepper.
4 lbs. raisins seeded and cut in pieces.	Salt to taste.

Cover meat and suet with boiling water and cook until tender, cool in water in which they were cooked; the suet will rise to top, forming a cake of fat, which may be easily removed. Finely chop meat, and add it to twice the amount of finely chopped apples. The apples should be quartered, cored, and pared, previous to chopping, or skins may be left on, which is not an objection if apples are finely chopped. Add quinces finely chopped, sugar, molasses, cider, raisins, currants, and citron; also suet, and stock in which meat and suet were cooked, reduced to one and one-half cups. Heat gradually, stir occasionally, and cook slowly two hours; then add brandy and spices.

English Mince Meat.

5 lbs. raisins seeded.	5 lbs. currants.
5 lbs. suet,	5 lbs. light brown sugar.
5 lbs. apples,	½ teaspoon mace.
4 lbs. citron,	finely chopped.	½ teaspoon cinnamon.
1½ lbs. blanched almonds,	2½ cups brandy.

Cook raisins, suet, apples, citron, currants, and sugar slowly for one and one-half hours; then add almonds, spices, and brandy.

Mince Meat (without Liquor).

Mix together one cup chopped apple, one-half cup raisins seeded and chopped, one-half cup currants, one-fourth cup butter, one tablespoon molasses, one tablespoon boiled cider, one cup sugar, one teaspoon cinnamon, one-half teaspoon cloves, one-half nutmeg grated, one salt-spoon of mace, and one teaspoon salt. Add enough stock in which meat was cooked to moisten; heat gradually to boiling point and simmer one hour; then add one cup chopped meat and two tablespoons Barberry Jelly. Cook fifteen minutes.

Mock Mince Pie.

4 common crackers rolled.	1 cup raisins seeded and
1½ cups sugar.	chopped.
1 cup molasses.	½ cup butter.
⅓ cup lemon juice or vinegar.	2 eggs well beaten.

Spices.

Mix ingredients in order given, adding spices to taste. Bake between crusts. This quantity will make two pies.

Peach Pie.

Remove skins from peaches. This may be done easily after allowing peaches to stand in boiling water one minute. Cut in eighths, cook until soft with enough water to prevent burning; sweeten to taste. Cool, and fill crust previously baked. Cover with whipped cream, sweetened and flavored.

Prune Pie.

½ lb. prunes.	1 tablespoon lemon juice.
½ cup sugar (scant).	1½ teaspoons butter.

1 tablespoon flour.

Wash prunes and soak in enough cold water to cover. Cook in same water until soft. Remove stones, cut prunes in quarters, and mix with sugar and lemon juice. Reduce liquor to one and one-half tablespoons. Line plate with paste, cover with prunes, pour over liquor, dot over with butter, and dredge with flour. Bake with an upper crust.

Rhubarb Pie.

1½ cups rhubarb.	1 egg.
⅞ cup sugar.	2 tablespoons flour.

Skin and cut stalks of rhubarb in half-inch pieces before measuring. Mix sugar, flour, and egg; add to rhubarb and bake between crusts. Many prefer to scald rhubarb before using; if so prepared, losing some of its acidity, less sugar is required.

Squash Pie.

1¼ cups steamed and strained squash.	¼ teaspoon cinnamon, ginger, nutmeg, or
¼ cup sugar.	½ teaspoon lemon extract.
½ teaspoon salt.	1 egg.
	⅞ cup milk.

Mix sugar, salt, and spice or extract, add squash, egg slightly beaten, and milk gradually. Bake in one crust, following directions for Custard Pie. If a richer pie is desired, use one cup squash, one-half cup each of milk and cream, and an additional egg yolk.

Pumpkin Pie.

Pumpkin Pie is made same as Squash Pie, using pumpkin in place of squash.

CHAPTER VIII.

PASTRY DESSERTS.

Banbury Tarts.

1 cup raisins.	1 egg.
1 cup sugar.	1 cracker.

Juice and grated rind 1 lemon.

Stone and chop raisins, add sugar, egg slightly beaten, cracker finely rolled, and lemon juice and rind. Roll pastry one-eighth inch thick, and cut pieces three and one-half inches long by three inches wide. Put two teaspoons of mixture on each piece. Moisten edge with cold water half-way round, fold over, press edges together with three-tined fork, first dipped in flour. Bake twenty minutes in slow oven.

Cheese Cakes.

1 cup sweet milk.	Juice and grated rind 1 lemon.
1 cup sour milk.	¼ cup almonds blanched and
1 cup sugar.	chopped.
Yolks 4 eggs.	¼ teaspoon salt.

Scald sweet and sour milk, strain through cheese cloth. To curd add sugar, yolks of eggs slightly beaten, lemon, and salt. Line patty pans with paste, fill with mixture, and sprinkle with chopped almonds. Bake until mixture is firm to the touch.

Cheese Straws.

Roll puff or plain paste one-fourth inch thick, sprinkle one-half with grated cheese to which has been added few grains of salt and cayenne. Fold, press edges firmly together, fold again, pat and roll out one-fourth inch thick. Sprinkle with cheese and proceed as before; repeat twice. Cut in strips five inches long and one-fourth inch wide. Bake eight minutes in hot oven. Parmesan cheese or equal parts of Parmesan and Edam cheese may be used. Cheese straws are piled log cabin fashion and served with cheese or salad course.

Condés.

Whites 2 eggs.   ¾ cup powdered sugar.
2 oz. almonds, blanched and finely chopped.

Beat whites of eggs until stiff, add sugar gradually, then almonds. Roll paste and cut in strips three and one-half inches long by one and one-half inches wide. Spread with mixture; avoid having it come close to edge. Dust with powdered sugar and bake fifteen minutes in moderate oven.

Cream Horns.

Roll puff paste in a long rectangular piece, one-eighth inch thick. Cut in strips three-fourths inch wide. Roll paste over wooden forms bought for the purpose, having edges overlap. Bake in hot oven until well puffed and slightly browned. Brush over with white of egg slightly beaten, diluted with one teaspoon water, then sprinkle with sugar. Return to oven and finish cooking, and remove from forms. When cold, fill with Cream Filling or whipped cream sweetened and flavored.

Florentine Meringue.

Roll puff or plain paste one-eighth inch thick; cut a piece ten inches long by seven inches wide; place on a sheet, wet edges, and put on a half-inch rim. Prick with fork six times, and bake in hot oven. Cool and spread with jam, cover with Meringue II., and almonds blanched and shredded, sprinkle with powdered sugar, and bake.

Napoleons.

Bake three sheets of pastry, pricking before baking. Put between the sheets Cream Filling; spread top with Confectioners' Frosting, crease in pieces about two and one-half by four inches, and cut with sharp knife.

Orange Sticks.

Cut puff or plain paste rolled one-eighth inch thick in strips five inches long by one inch wide, and bake in hot oven. Put together in pairs, with Orange Filling between

Lemon Sticks.

Lemon Sticks may be made in same manner as Orange Sticks, using Lemon Filling.

Palm Leaves.

Roll remnants of puff paste one-eighth inch thick; sprinkle one-half surface with powdered sugar, fold, press edges together, pat and roll out, using sugar for dredging board; repeat three times. After the last rolling fold four times. The pastry should be in long strip one and one-half inches wide. From the end, cut pieces one-inch wide; place on baking-sheet, broad side down, one-inch apart, and separate layers of pastry at one end to suggest a leaf. Bake eight minutes in hot oven; these will spread while baking.

Raspberry Puffs.

Roll plain paste one-eighth inch thick, and cut in pieces four by three and one-half inches. Put one-half tablespoon raspberry jam on centre of lower half of each piece, wet edges half-way around, fold, press edges firmly together, prick tops, place on sheet, and bake twenty minutes in hot oven. Mince meat or apple sauce may be used for filling.

Tarts.

Roll puff paste one-eighth inch thick. Shape with a fluted round cutter, first dipped in flour; with a smaller cutter remove centres from half the pieces, leaving rings one-half inch wide. Brush with cold water the larger pieces near the edge; fit on rings, pressing lightly. Chill thoroughly, and bake fifteen minutes in hot oven. By brushing tops of rings with beaten yolk of egg diluted with one teaspoonful water, they will have a glazed appearance. Cool, and fill with jam or jelly.

Polish Tartlets.

Roll puff or plain paste one-eighth inch thick, and cut in two and one-half inch squares; wet the corners, fold toward the centre, and press lightly; bake on a sheet; when cool, press down the centres and fill, using two-thirds quince marmalade and one-third currant jelly.

MERINGUES.

For Pies, Puddings, and Desserts.

Eggs for meringues should be thoroughly chilled, and beaten with silver fork, wire spoon or whisk. Where several eggs are needed, much time is saved by using a whisk. Meringues on pies, puddings, or desserts, may be spread evenly, spread and piled in the centre, put on lightly by spoonfuls, or spread evenly with part of the mixture, the remainder being forced through a pastry bag and tube.

Meringues I. and III. should be baked fifteen minutes in slow oven. Meringue II. should be cooked eight minutes in moderate oven; if removed from oven before cooked, the eggs will liquefy and meringue settle; if cooked too long, meringue is tough.

Meringue I.

Whites 2 eggs.   ½ tablespoon lemon juice or
2 tablespoons powdered sugar.   ¼ teaspoon vanilla.

Beat whites until stiff, add sugar gradually and continue beating, then add flavoring.

Meringue II.

Whites 3 eggs.   ½ teaspoon lemon extract or
7½ tablespoons powdered sugar.   ⅓ teaspoon vanilla.

Beat whites until stiff, add four tablespoons sugar gradually, and beat vigorously; fold in remaining sugar, and add flavoring.

Meringue III.

Whites 4 eggs.   ⅞ cup powdered sugar.
2 tablespoons lemon juice.

Put whites of eggs and sugar in bowl, beat mixture until stiff enough to hold its shape, add lemon juice drop by drop, continuing the beating. It will take thirty minutes to beat mixture sufficiently stiff to hold its shape, but when baked it makes a most delicious meringue.

Meringues Glacées, or Kisses.

Whites 4 eggs.   1¼ cups powdered sugar or
½ teaspoon vanilla.   1 cup fine granulated.

Beat whites until stiff, add gradually two-thirds of sugar, and continue beating until mixture will hold its shape; fold in remaining sugar, and add flavoring. Shape with a spoon or pastry bag and tube on wet board covered with letter paper. Bake thirty minutes in very slow oven, remove from paper and put together in pairs, or if intending to fill with whipped cream or ice cream remove soft part with spoon and place meringues in oven to dry.

Nut Meringues.

To Meringue Glacée mixture add chopped nut meat; almonds, English walnuts, or hickory nuts are preferred. Shape by dropping mixture from tip of spoon in small piles one-half inch apart, or by using pastry bag and tube. Sprinkle with nut meat and bake.

Meringues (Mushrooms).

Shape Meringue Glacée mixture in rounds the size of mushroom caps, using pastry bag and tube; sprinkle with grated chocolate. Shape stems like mushroom stems. Bake, remove from paper, and place caps on stems.

Meringues Panachées.

Fill Meringues Glacées with ice cream, or ice cream and water ice. Garnish with whipped cream forced through pastry bag and tube, and candied cherries.

CHAPTER IX.

GINGERBREADS, COOKIES, AND WAFERS.

Hot Water Gingerbread.

1 cup molasses.	1 teaspoon soda.
½ cup boiling water.	1½ teaspoons ginger.
2¼ cups flour.	½ teaspoon salt.

3 tablespoons melted butter.

Add water to molasses. Mix and sift dry ingredients, combine mixtures, add butter, and beat vigorously. Pour into a buttered shallow pan, and bake twenty-five minutes in a moderate oven. Chicken fat tried out and clarified furnishes an excellent shortening, and may be used in place of butter.

Sour Milk Gingerbread.

1 cup molasses.	1¾ teaspoons soda.
1 cup sour milk.	2 teaspoons ginger.
2⅓ cups flour.	½ teaspoon salt.

¼ cup melted butter.

Add milk to molasses. Mix and sift dry ingredients, combine mixtures, add butter, and beat vigorously. Pour into a buttered shallow pan, and bake twenty-five minutes in a moderate oven.

Soft Molasses Gingerbread.

1 cup molasses.	1 egg.
⅓ cup butter.	2 cups flour.
1¾ teaspoons soda.	2 teaspoons ginger
½ cup sour milk.	½ teaspoon salt.

Put butter and molasses in saucepan and cook until boiling point is reached. Remove from fire, add soda, and beat vigorously. Then add milk, egg well beaten, and remaining ingredients mixed and sifted. Bake fifteen minutes in buttered small tin pans, having pans two-thirds filled with mixture.

Cambridge Gingerbread.

⅓ cup butter.	1½ teaspoons soda.
⅔ cup boiling water.	½ teaspoon salt.
1 cup molasses.	1 teaspoon cinnamon.
1 egg.	1 teaspoon ginger.
3 cups flour.	¼ teaspoon clove.

Melt butter in water, add molasses, egg well beaten, and dry ingredients mixed and sifted. Bake in a buttered shallow pan.

Soft Sugar Gingerbread.

2 eggs.	3 teaspoons baking powder.
1 cup sugar.	½ teaspoon salt.
1¾ cups flour.	1½ teaspoons ginger.
⅔ cup thin cream.	

Beat eggs until light, and add sugar gradually. Mix and sift dry ingredients, and add alternately with cream to first mixture. Turn into a buttered cake pan, and bake thirty minutes in a moderate oven.

Gossamer Gingerbread.

⅓ cup butter.	½ cup milk.
1 cup sugar.	1⅞ cups flour.
1 egg.	3 teaspoons baking powder.
1 teaspoon yellow ginger.	

Cream the butter, add sugar gradually, then egg well beaten. Add milk, and dry ingredients mixed and sifted. Spread in a buttered dripping-pan as thinly as possible, using the back of mixing-spoon. Bake fifteen minutes. Sprinkle with sugar, and cut in small squares or diamonds before removing from pan.

Fairy Gingerbread.

½ cup butter.   ½ cup milk.
1 cup light brown sugar.   1⅞ cups bread flour.
2 teaspoons ginger.

Cream the butter, add sugar gradually, and milk very slowly.   Mix and sift flour and ginger, and combine mixtures.   Spread very thinly with a broad, long-bladed knife on a buttered, inverted dripping pan.   Bake in a moderate oven.   Cut in squares before removing from pan.   Watch carefully and turn pan frequently during baking, that all may be evenly cooked.   If mixture around edge of pan is cooked before that in the centre, pan should be removed from oven, cooked part cut off, and remainder returned to oven to finish cooking.

Hard Sugar Gingerbread.

¾ cup butter.   5 cups flour.
1½ cups sugar.   ¾ tablespoon baking powder.
¾ cup milk.   1½ teaspoons salt.
¾ tablespoon ginger.

Cream the butter, add sugar gradually, milk, and dry ingredients mixed and sifted.   Put some of mixture on an inverted dripping-pan and roll as thinly as possible to cover pan.   Mark dough with a coarse grater.   Sprinkle with sugar and bake in a moderate oven.   Before removing from pan, cut in strips four and one-half inches long by one and one-half inches wide.

Molasses Drop Cakes.

1 cup molasses.   1 cup hot water.
½ cup melted butter.   1 egg.
1 cup sugar.   2 teaspoons ginger.
2 teaspoons soda.   ½ teaspoon salt.
4 cups flour.

Mix molasses, butter, and sugar.   Add soda and beat thoroughly, then add water, egg well beaten, and flour mixed and sifted with ginger and salt. Drop by spoonfuls on a buttered sheet. Bake twelve to fifteen minutes in a hot oven.

Ginger Snaps.

1 cup molasses.	½ teaspoon soda.
½ cup shortening.	1 tablespoon ginger.
3¼ cups flour.	1½ teaspoons salt.

Heat molasses to boiling point and pour over shortening. Add dry ingredients mixed and sifted. Chill thoroughly. Toss one-fourth of mixture on a floured board and roll as thinly as possible; shape with a small round cutter, first dipped in flour. Place near together on a buttered sheet and bake in a moderate oven. Gather up the trimmings and roll with another portion of dough. During rolling, the bowl containing mixture should be kept in a cool place, or it will be necessary to add more flour to dough, which makes cookies hard rather than crisp and short.

Molasses Cookies.

1 cup molasses.	1 tablespoon ginger.
½ cup shortening, butter and lard mixed.	1 tablespoon soda.
	2 tablespoons warm milk.
2 cups bread flour.	

Heat molasses to boiling point, add shortening, ginger, soda dissolved in warm milk, and flour. Proceed as for Ginger Snaps.

Soft Molasses Cookies.

1 cup molasses.	½ cup shortening melted.
1¾ teaspoons soda.	2 teaspoons ginger.
1 cup sour milk.	1 teaspoon salt.
Flour.	

Add soda to molasses and beat thoroughly; add milk, shortening, ginger, salt, and flour. Enough flour must be used to make mixture of right consistency to drop easily from spoon. Let stand several hours in a cold place to thoroughly chill. Toss one-half mixture at a time on slightly floured board and roll lightly to one-fourth inch thickness. Shape with a round cutter, first dipped in flour. Bake on a buttered sheet.

Spice Cookies.

½ cup molasses.	2 cups flour.
¼ cup sugar.	½ teaspoon soda.
1½ tablespoons butter.	½ teaspoon salt.
1½ tablespoons lard.	⅛ teaspoon clove.
1 tablespoon milk.	½ teaspoon cinnamon.

½ teaspoon nutmeg.

Heat molasses to boiling point. Add sugar, shortening, and milk. Mix and sift dry ingredients, and add to first mixture. Chill, and proceed as with Ginger Snaps.

Scotch Wafers.

1 cup fine oatmeal.	1 teaspoon salt.
1 cup Quaker Rolled Oats	⅛ teaspoon soda.
2 cups flour.	¼ cup butter or lard.
¼ cup sugar.	½ cup hot water.

Mix first six ingredients. Melt shortening in water and add to first mixture. Toss on a floured board, pat and roll as thinly as possible. Shape with a cutter, or with a sharp knife cut in strips. Bake on a buttered sheet in a slow oven. These are well adapted for children's luncheons, and are much enjoyed by the convalescent, taken with a glass of milk.

Oatmeal Cookies.

1 egg.	½ cup fine oatmeal.
¼ cup sugar.	2 cups flour.
¼ cup thin cream.	2 teaspoons baking powder.
¼ cup milk.	1 teaspoon salt.

Beat egg until light, add sugar, cream, and milk; then add oatmeal, flour, baking powder, and salt, mixed and sifted. Toss on a floured board, roll, cut in shape, and bake in a moderate oven.

Vanilla Wafers.

⅓ cup butter and lard in
    equal proportions.
1 cup sugar.
1 egg.

¼ cup milk.
2 cups flour.
2 teaspoons baking powder.
½ teaspoon salt.

2 teaspoons vanilla.

Cream the butter, add sugar, egg well beaten, milk, and vanilla. Mix and sift dry ingredients and add to first mixture. Proceed as with Ginger Snaps.

Cream Cookies.

⅓ cup butter.
1 cup sugar.
2 eggs.
½ cup thin cream.

2 teaspoons baking powder.
1 teaspoon salt.
2 teaspoons yellow ginger.
Flour to roll.

Mix and bake same as Vanilla Wafers.

Imperial Cookies.

½ cup butter.
1 cup sugar.
2 eggs.
1 tablespoon milk.

2¾ cups flour.
2 teaspoons baking powder.
½ teaspoon lemon extract.
½ teaspoon grated nutmeg.

Mix and bake same as Vanilla Wafers.

Hermits.

⅓ cup butter.
⅔ cup sugar.
1 egg.
2 tablespoons milk.
2 cups flour.
2 teaspoons baking powder.

⅓ cup raisins stoned and cut
    in small pieces.
½ teaspoon cinnamon.
¼ teaspoon clove.
¼ teaspoon mace.
¼ teaspoon nutmeg.

Cream the butter, add sugar gradually, then raisins, egg well beaten, and milk. Mix and sift dry ingredients and add to first mixture. Roll mixture a little thicker than for Vanilla Wafers.

Boston Cookies.

1 cup butter.	½ teaspoon salt.
1½ cups sugar.	1 teaspoon cinnamon.
3 eggs.	1 cup chopped nut meat,
1 teaspoon soda.	hickory or English walnut.
1½ tablespoons hot water.	½ cup currants.
3¼ cups flour.	½ cup raisins seeded and
	chopped.

Cream the butter, add sugar gradually, and eggs well beaten. Add soda dissolved in water, one-half flour mixed and sifted with salt and cinnamon; then add nut meat, fruit, and remaining flour. Drop by spoonfuls one inch apart on a buttered sheet, and bake in a moderate oven.

Cocoanut Cream Cookies.

2 eggs.	½ cup shredded cocoanut.
1 cup sugar.	3 cups flour.
1 cup thick cream.	3 teaspoons baking powder.
1 teaspoon salt.	

Beat eggs until light, add sugar gradually, cocoanut, cream, and flour mixed and sifted with baking powder. Chill, toss on a floured board, pat and roll one-half inch thick. Sprinkle with cocoanut, roll one-fourth inch thick, and shape with a small round cutter, first dipped in flour. Bake on a buttered sheet.

Peanut Cookies.

2 tablespoons butter.	¼ teaspoon salt.
¼ cup sugar.	½ cup flour.
1 egg.	2 tablespoons milk.
1 teaspoon baking powder.	½ cup finely chopped peanuts.
½ teaspoon lemon juice.	

Cream the butter, add sugar, and egg well beaten. Mix and sift baking powder, salt, and flour; add to first mixture; then add milk, peanuts, and lemon juice. Drop from a teaspoon on an unbuttered sheet one-inch apart, and place one-half peanut on top of each. Bake twelve to fifteen minutes in a slow oven. This recipe will make twenty-four cookies.

Seed Cakes.

Follow recipe for Cocoanut Cream Cookies, using one and one-half tablespoons caraway seeds in place of cocoanut.

Chocolate Cookies.

½ cup butter.	2 oz. Baker's chocolate.
1 cup sugar.	2½ cups flour (scant).
1 egg.	2 teaspoons baking powder.
¼ teaspoon salt.	¼ cup milk.

Cream the butter, add sugar gradually, egg well beaten, salt, and chocolate melted. Beat well, and add flour mixed and sifted with baking powder alternately with milk. Chill, roll very thin, then shape with a small cutter, first dipped in flour, and bake in a hot oven.

Sand Tarts.

½ cup butter.	2 teaspoons baking powder.
1 cup sugar.	White 1 egg.
1 egg.	Blanched almonds.
1½ cups flour.	1 tablespoon sugar.
¼ teaspoon cinnamon.	

Cream the butter, add sugar gradually, and egg well beaten; then add flour mixed and sifted with baking powder. Chill, toss one-half mixture on a floured board, and roll one-eighth inch thick. Shape with a doughnut cutter. Brush over with white of egg, and sprinkle with sugar mixed with cinnamon. Split almonds, and arrange three halves on each at equal distances. Place on a buttered sheet, and bake eight minutes in a slow oven.

Rolled Wafers tied in bundles of three with baby ribbon.

Rolled Wafers.

¼ cup butter.   ¼ cup milk.
½ cup powdered sugar.   ⅞ cup bread flour.
                 ½ teaspoon vanilla.

Cream the butter, add sugar gradually, and milk drop by drop; then add flour and flavoring. Spread very thinly with a broad, long-bladed knife on a buttered inverted dripping pan. Crease in three-inch squares, and bake in a slow oven until delicately browned. Place pan on back of range, cut squares apart with a sharp knife, and roll while warm in tubular or cornucopia shape. If squares become too brittle to roll, place in oven to soften. If rolled tubular shape, tie in bunches with narrow ribbon. These are very attractive, and may be served with sherbet, ice cream, or chocolate. If rolled cornucopia shape, they may be filled with whipped cream just before sending to table. Colored wafers may be made from this mixture by adding leaf green or fruit red. If colored green, flavor with one-fourth teaspoon almond and three-fourths teaspoon vanilla. If colored pink, flavor with rose. Colored wafers must be baked in a very slow oven to prevent browning.

Almond Wafers tied together with ribbon.

Almond Wafers.

Before baking Rolled Wafers, sprinkle with almonds blanched and chopped.

CHAPTER X.

CAKE.

THE mixing and baking of cake requires more care and judgment than any other branch of cookery; notwithstanding, it seems the one most frequently attempted by the inexperienced.

Two kinds of cake mixtures are considered: —

I. Without butter.   Example: Sponge Cakes.

II. With butter.   Examples: Cup and Pound Cakes.

In cake making (1) the best ingredients are essential; (2) great care must be taken in measuring and combining ingredients; (3) pans must be properly prepared; (4) oven heat must be regulated, and cake watched during baking.

Best tub butter, fine granulated sugar, fresh eggs, and pastry flour are essentials for good cake.   Coarse granulated sugar, bought by so many, if used in cake making, gives a coarse texture and hard crust.   Pastry flour contains more starch and less gluten than bread flour, therefore makes a lighter, more tender cake.   If bread flour must be used, allow two tablespoons less for each cup than the recipe calls for.   Flours differ greatly in thickening properties; for this reason it is always well when using from a new bag to try a small cake, as the amount of flour given may not make the perfect loaf.   In winter, cake may be made of less flour than in summer.

Before attempting to mix cake, study How to Measure and How to Combine Ingredients.

Look at the fire, and replenish by sprinkling on a small quantity of coal if there is not sufficient heat to effect the baking.

To Mix Sponge Cake.   Separate yolks from whites of eggs.   Beat yolks until thick and lemon colored, using an egg beater; add sugar gradually, and continue beating; then add flavoring.   Beat whites until stiff and dry, — when they will fly from the beater, — and add to the first mixture.   Mix and sift flour with salt, and cut and fold in at the last.   If mixture is beaten after the addition of flour, much of the work already done of enclosing a large amount of air will be undone by breaking air bubbles.   These rules apply to a mixture where baking powder is not employed.

To Mix Butter Cakes.   An earthen bowl should always be used for mixing cake, and a wooden cake-spoon with slits lightens the labor.   Measure dry ingredients, and mix and sift baking powder and spices, if used, with flour.   Count out number of eggs required, breaking each separately that there may be no loss should a stale egg chance to be found in the number, separating yolks from whites if rule so specifies.   Measure butter, then liquid.   Having everything in readiness, the mixing may be quickly accomplished.   If butter is very hard, by allowing it to stand a short time in a warm room it is measured and creamed much easier.   If time cannot be allowed for this to be done, warm bowl by pouring in some hot water, letting stand one minute, then emptying and wiping dry.   Avoid overheating bowl, as butter will become oily rather than creamy.   Put butter in bowl, and cream by working with a wooden spoon until soft and of a creamy consistency; then add sugar gradually, and continue beating.   Add yolks of eggs or whole eggs beaten until light, liquid, and flour mixed and sifted with baking powder; or liquid and flour may be added alternately.   When yolks and whites of eggs are beaten separately, whites are usually added at the last, as is the case when whites of eggs alone are used.   A cake can be made fine grained only by long beating, although light and delicate with a small amount of beating.   Never stir cake after the final beating, remembering that beating motion should always be the last used. Fruit, when added to cake, is usually floured to prevent its settling to the bottom. This is not necessary if it is added directly after the sugar, which is desirable in all dark cakes. If a light fruit cake is made, fruit added in this way discolors the loaf. Citron is first cut in thin slices, then in strips, floured, and put in between layers of cake mixtures. Raisins are seeded and cut, rather than chopped. *To seed raisins*, wet tips of fingers in a cup of warm water. Then break skins with fingers, or cut with a vegetable knife; remove seeds, and put in cup of water. This is better than covering raisins with warm water; if this be done, water clings to fruit, and when dredged with flour a pasty mass is formed on the outside. Washed currants, put up in packages, are quite free from stems and foreign substances, and need only picking over and rolling in flour. Currants bought in bulk need thorough cleaning. First roll in flour, which helps to start dirt; wash in cold water, drain, and spread to dry; then roll again in flour before using.

To Butter and Fill Pans. Grease pans with melted fat, applying the same with a butter brush. If butter is used, put in a small saucepan and place on back of range; when melted, salt will settle to the bottom; butter is then called *clarified*. Just before putting in mixture, dredge pans thoroughly with flour, invert, and shake pan to remove all superflous flour, leaving only a thin coating which adheres to butter. This gives to cake a smooth under surface, which is especially desirable if cake is to be frosted. Pans may be lined with paper. If this is done, paper should just cover bottom of pan and project over sides. Then ends of pan and paper are buttered.

In filling pans, have the mixture come well to the corners and sides of pans, leaving a slight depression in the centre, and when baked the cake will be perfectly flat on top. Cake pans should be filled nearly two-thirds full if cake is expected to rise to top of pan.

To Bake Cake. The baking of cake is more critical than the mixing. Many a well-mixed cake has been spoiled in the baking. No oven thermometer has yet proved practical, and although many teachers of cookery have given oven tests, experience alone has proved the most reliable teacher. In baking cake, divide the time required into quarters. During the first quarter the mixture should begin to rise; second quarter, continue rising and begin to brown; third quarter, continue browning; fourth quarter, finish baking and shrink from pan. If oven is too hot, open check and raise back covers, or leave oven door ajar. It is sometimes necessary to cover cake with brown paper; there is, however, danger of cake adhering to paper. Cake should be often looked at during baking, and providing oven door is opened and closed carefully, there is no danger of this causing cake to fall. Cake should not be moved in oven until it has risen its full height; after this time it is usually desirable to move it that it may be evenly browned. Cake when done shrinks from the pan, and in most cases this is a sufficient test; however, in pound cakes this rule does not apply. Pound and rich fruit cakes are tested by pressing surface with tip of finger. If cake feels firm to touch and follows finger back into place, it is safe to remove it from the oven. When baking cake arrange to have nothing else in the oven, and place loaf or loaves as near the centre of oven as possible. If placed close to fire box, one side of loaf is apt to become burned before sufficiently risen to turn. If cake is put in too slow an oven, it often rises over sides of pan and is of very coarse texture; if put in too hot an oven, it browns on top before sufficiently risen, and in its attempt to rise breaks through the crust, thus making an unsightly loaf. Cake will also crack on top if too much flour has been used. The oven should be kept at as nearly uniform temperature as possible. Small and layer cakes require a hotter oven than loaf cakes.

To Remove Cake from Pans. Remove cake from pans as soon as it comes from the oven, by inverting pan on a wire cake cooler, or on a board covered with a piece of old linen. If cake is inclined to stick, do not hurry it from pan, but loosen with knife around edges, and rest pan on its four sides successively, thus by its own weight cake may be helped out.

To Frost Cake. Where cooked frostings are used, it makes but little difference whether they are spread on hot or cold cake. Where uncooked frostings are used, it is best to have the cake slightly warm, with the exception of Confectioners' Frosting, where boiling water is employed.

Hot Water Sponge Cake.

Yolks 2 eggs.	Whites 2 eggs.
1 cup sugar.	1 cup flour.
⅜ cup hot water.	1½ teaspoons baking powder.
¼ teaspoon lemon extract.	¼ teaspoon salt.

Beat yolks of eggs until thick and lemon-colored, add one-half the sugar gradually, and continue beating; then add water, remaining sugar, lemon extract, whites of eggs beaten until stiff, and flour mixed and sifted with baking powder and salt. Bake twenty-five minutes in a moderate oven in a buttered and floured shallow pan.

Cheap Sponge Cake.

Yolks 3 eggs.	1½ teaspoons baking powder.
1 cup sugar.	¼ teaspoon salt.
1 tablespoon hot water.	Whites 3 eggs.
1 cup flour.	2 teaspoons vinegar.

Beat yolks of eggs until thick and lemon-colored, add sugar gradually, and continue beating; then add water, flour mixed and sifted with baking powder and salt, whites of eggs beaten until stiff, and vinegar. Bake thirty-five minutes in a moderate oven, in a buttered and floured cake pan.

Cream Sponge Cake.

Yolks 4 eggs.	Flour.
1 cup sugar.	1½ teaspoons baking powder.
3 tablespoons cold water.	¼ teaspoon salt.
1½ tablespoons corn-starch.	Whites 4 eggs.

1 teaspoon lemon extract.

Beat yolks of eggs until thick and lemon-colored, add sugar gradually, and beat two minutes; then add water. Put corn-starch in a cup and fill cup with flour. Mix and sift corn-starch and flour with baking powder and salt, and add to first mixture. When thoroughly mixed add whites of eggs beaten until stiff, and flavoring. Bake thirty minutes in a moderate oven.

Sponge Cake.

Yolks 6 eggs.	Grated rind one-half lemon.
1 cup sugar.	Whites 6 eggs.
1 tablespoon lemon juice.	1 cup flour.

¼ teaspoon salt.

Beat yolks until thick and lemon-colored, add sugar gradually, and continue beating, using Dover egg-beater. Add lemon-juice, rind, and whites of eggs beaten until stiff and dry. When whites are partially mixed with yolks, remove beater, and carefully cut and fold in flour mixed and sifted with salt. Bake one hour in a slow oven, in an angel cake pan or deep narrow pan.

Genuine sponge cake contains no rising properties, but is made light by the quantity of air beaten into both yolks and whites of eggs, and the expansion of that air in baking. It requires a slow oven. All so-called sponge cakes which have the addition of soda and cream of tartar or baking powder require same oven temperature as butter cakes. When failures are made in Sunshine and Angel Cake, they are usually traced to baking in too slow an oven, and removing from oven before thoroughly cooked.

Sunshine Cake.

Whites 10 eggs.	1 teaspoon lemon extract.
1½ cups powdered sugar.	1 cup flour.
Yolks 6 eggs.	1 teaspoon cream of tartar.

Beat whites of eggs until stiff and dry, add sugar gradually, and continue beating; then add yolks of eggs beaten until thick and lemon colored, and extract. Cut and fold in flour mixed and sifted with cream of tartar. Bake fifty minutes in a moderate oven in an angel cake pan.

Angel Cake.

1 cup white of eggs.	⅓ cup flour.
¾ cup sugar.	½ teaspoon salt.
¼ cup corn-starch.	1 teaspoon cream of tartar.
1 teaspoon vanilla.	

Beat whites of eggs until stiff and dry, add sugar gradually and continue beating, then add flavoring. Cut and fold in corn-starch, flour, salt, and cream of tartar, mixed and sifted. Bake forty-five to fifty minutes in an unbuttered angel cake pan in a moderate oven.

Lady Fingers.

Whites 3 eggs.	⅓ cup of flour.
⅓ cup powdered sugar.	⅛ teaspoon salt.
Yolks 2 eggs.	¼ teaspoon vanilla.

Beat whites of eggs until stiff and dry, add sugar gradually, and continue beating. Then add yolks of eggs beaten until thick and lemon colored, and flavoring. Cut and fold in flour mixed and sifted with salt. Shape four and one-half inches long and one inch wide on a tin sheet covered with unbuttered paper, using a pastry bag and tube. Sprinkle with powdered sugar, and bake eight minutes in a moderate oven. Remove from paper with a knife. Lady Fingers are much used for lining moulds that are to be filled with whipped cream mixtures. They are often served with frozen desserts, and sometimes put together in pairs with a thin coating of whipped cream between, when they are attractive for children's parties.

Sponge Drop.

Drop Lady Finger mixture from tip of spoon on unbuttered paper. Sprinkle with powdered sugar, and bake eight minutes in a moderate oven.

Jelly Roll.

3 eggs.	1 teaspoon baking powder.
1 cup sugar.	¼ teaspoon salt.
½ tablespoon milk.	1 cup flour.

1 tablespoon melted butter.

Beat egg until light, add sugar gradually, milk, flour mixed and sifted with baking powder and salt, then butter. Line the bottom of a dripping-pan with paper; butter paper and sides of pan. Cover bottom of pan with mixture, and spread evenly. Bake twelve minutes in a moderate oven. Take from oven and turn on a paper sprinkled with powdered sugar. Quickly remove paper, and cut off a thin strip from sides and ends of cake. Spread with jelly or jam which has been beaten to consistency to spread easily, and roll. After cake has been rolled, roll paper around cake that it may better keep in shape. The work must be done quickly, or cake will crack in rolling.

Aunt Caddie's Cake.

¼ cup butter.	1 teaspoon salt.
½ cup sugar.	1 teaspoon cinnamon.
1 cup molasses.	⅓ teaspoon clove.
1 cup sour milk.	3 cups flour.
1½ teaspoons soda.	¾ cup raisins seeded and cut in pieces.

Cream the butter, add sugar gradually, molasses, sour milk, and raisins. Mix and sift remaining ingredients, and combine mixtures. Bake fifty minutes in a deep pan.

Election Cake.

½ cup butter.	8 finely chopped figs.
1 cup bread dough.	1¼ cups flour.
1 egg.	½ teaspoon soda.
1 cup brown sugar.	1 teaspoon cinnamon.
½ cup sour milk.	¼ teaspoon clove.
⅔ cup raisins seeded and	¼ teaspoon mace.
cut in pieces.	¼ teaspoon nutmeg.

1 teaspoon salt.

Work butter into dough, using the hand. Add egg well beaten, sugar, milk, fruit dredged with two tablespoons flour, and flour mixed and sifted with remaining ingredients. Put into a well-buttered bread pan, cover, and let rise one and one-fourth hours. Bake one hour in a slow oven. Cover with Boiled Milk Frosting.

One Egg Cake.

¼ cup of butter.	½ cup of milk.
½ cup sugar.	1½ cups flour.
1 egg.	2½ teaspoons baking powder.

Cream the butter, add sugar gradually, and egg well beaten. Mix and sift flour and baking powder, add alternately with milk to first mixture. Bake thirty minutes in a shallow pan. Spread with Chocolate Frosting.

Chocolate Cake.

½ cup butter.	1⅓ cups flour.
1 cup sugar.	2½ teaspoons baking powder.
2 small eggs.	2 oz. chocolate, melted.
½ cup milk.	½ teaspoon vanilla.

Cream the butter, add sugar gradually, and yolks eggs well beaten, then whites eggs beaten until stiff. Add milk, flour mixed and sifted with baking powder, and beat thoroughly. Then add chocolate and vanilla. Bake forty minutes in a shallow cake pan.

Chocolate Nougat Cake.

¼ cup butter.
1½ cups powdered sugar.
1 egg.
1 cup milk.
2 cups bread flour.

3 teaspoons baking powder.
½ teaspoon vanilla.
2 squares chocolate melted.
⅓ cup powdered sugar.
⅔ cup almonds blanched
and shredded.

Cream the butter, add gradually one and one-half cups sugar, and egg unbeaten; when well mixed, add two-thirds milk, flour mixed and sifted with baking powder, and vanilla. To melted chocolate add one-third cup powdered sugar, place on range, add gradually remaining milk, and cook until smooth. Cool slightly, and add to cake mixture. Bake fifteen to twenty minutes in round layer cake pans. Put between layers and on top of cake White Mountain Cream sprinkled with almonds.

Cream Pie I.

⅓ cup butter.
1 cup sugar.
2 eggs.

½ cup milk.
1¾ cups flour.
2½ teaspoons baking powder.

Mix as One Egg Cake. Bake in round layer cake pans. Put Cream Filling between layers and sprinkle top with powdered sugar.

Cream Pie II.

Make as Cream Pie I., using French Cream Filling in place of Cream Filling.

Cocoanut Pie.

Mix and bake as Cream Pie. Put Cocoanut Filling between layers and on top.

Washington Pie.

Mix and bake as Cream Pie. Put raspberry jam or jelly between layers and sprinkle top with powdered sugar.

Chocolate Pie.

2 tablespoons butter.	½ cup milk.
¾ cup sugar.	1⅓ cups flour.
1 egg.	2 teaspoons baking powder.

Mix and bake as Cream Pie. Split layers, and spread between and on top of each a thin layer of Chocolate Frosting.

Orange Cake.

¼ cup butter.	½ cup milk.
1 cup sugar.	1⅔ cups flour.
2 eggs.	2½ teaspoons baking powder.

Cream the butter, add sugar gradually, eggs well beaten, and milk. Then add flour mixed and sifted with baking powder. Bake in a thin sheet in a dripping-pan. Cut in halves, spread one-half with Orange Filling. Put over other half, and cover with Orange Frosting.

Quick Cake.

⅓ cup soft butter.	1¾ cups flour.
1⅓ cups brown sugar.	3 teaspoons baking powder.
2 eggs.	½ teaspoon cinnamon.
½ cup milk.	½ teaspoon grated nutmeg.

½ lb. dates stoned and cut in pieces.

Put ingredients in a bowl and beat all together for three minutes. Bake in a cake pan thirty-five to forty minutes. If directions are followed this makes a most satisfactory cake; but if ingredients are added separately it will not prove a success.

Boston Favorite Cake.

⅔ cup butter.	1 cup milk.
2 cups sugar.	3½ cups flour.
4 eggs.	5 teaspoons baking powder.

Cream the butter, add sugar gradually, eggs beaten until light, then milk and flour mixed and sifted with baking powder. This recipe makes two loaves.

Cream Cake.

2 eggs.	2½ teaspoons baking powder.
1 cup sugar.	½ teaspoon salt.
⅔ cup thin cream.	½ teaspoon cinnamon.
1⅔ cups flour.	¼ teaspoon mace.

¼ teaspoon ginger.

Put unbeaten eggs in a bowl, add sugar and cream, and beat vigorously. Mix and sift remaining ingredients, then add to first mixture. Bake thirty minutes in a shallow cake pan.

Currant Cake.

½ cup butter.	½ cup milk.
1 cup sugar.	2 cups flour.
2 eggs.	3 teaspoons baking powder.
Yolk 1 egg.	1 cup currants mixed with
	1 tablespoon flour.

Cream the butter, add sugar gradually, and eggs and egg yolk well beaten. Then add milk, flour mixed and sifted with baking powder, and currants. Bake forty minutes in a buttered and floured cake pan.

Velvet Cake.

½ cup butter.	1½ cups flour.
1½ cups sugar.	½ cup corn-starch.
Yolks 4 eggs.	4 teaspoons baking powder.
½ cup cold water.	Whites 4 eggs.

⅓ cup almonds blanched and shredded.

Cream the butter, add sugar gradually, yolks of eggs well beaten, and water. Mix and sift flour, corn-starch, and baking powder, and add to first mixture; then add whites of eggs beaten until stiff. After putting in pan, cover with almonds and sprinkle with powdered sugar. Bake forty minutes in a moderate oven.

Walnut Cake.

½ cup butter.
1 cup sugar.
Yolks 3 eggs.
½ cup milk.

1¾ cups flour.
2½ teaspoons baking powder.
Whites 2 eggs.
¾ cup walnut meat broken in pieces.

Mix ingredients in order given. Bake forty-five minutes in a moderate oven. Cover with White Mountain Cream, crease in squares, and put one-half walnut on each square.

Spanish Cake.

½ cup butter.
1 cup sugar.
Yolks 2 eggs.
½ cup milk.

1¾ cups flour.
3 teaspoons baking powder.
1 teaspoon cinnamon.
Whites 2 eggs.

Mix ingredients in order given. Bake in shallow tins and spread between and on top Caramel Frosting.

Cup Cake.

⅔ cup butter.
2 cups sugar.
4 eggs.

1 cup milk.
3¼ cups flour.
4 teaspoons baking powder.

¼ teaspoon mace.

Put butter and sugar in a bowl, and stir until well mixed; add eggs well beaten, then milk, and flour mixed and sifted with baking powder and mace. Bake in individual tins. Cover with Chocolate Frosting.

Brownies.

⅓ cup butter.
⅓ cup powdered sugar.
⅓ cup Porto Rico molasses.

1 egg well beaten.
⅞ cup bread flour.
1 cup pecan meat cut in pieces.

Mix ingredients in order given. Bake in small, shallow fancy cake tins, garnishing top of each cake with one-half pecan.

Ribbon Cake.

½ cup butter.
2 cups sugar.
Yolks 4 eggs.
1 cup milk.
3½ cups flour.
5 teaspoons baking powder.
Whites 4 eggs.

½ teaspoon cinnamon.
¼ teaspoon mace.
¼ teaspoon nutmeg.
⅓ cup raisins seeded and
 cut in pieces.
⅓ cup figs finely chopped.
1 tablespoon molasses.

Mix first seven ingredients in order given. Bake two-thirds of the mixture in two layer cake pans. To the remainder add spices, fruit, and molasses, and bake in a layer cake pan. Put layers together with jelly (apple usually being preferred as it has less flavor), having the dark layer in the centre.

Coffee Cake.

¼ cup butter.
½ cup sugar.
½ cup raisins seeded and
 cut in pieces.
½ cup molasses.
¼ cup boiled coffee.

2 eggs.
2½ cups flour.
3 teaspoons baking powder.
½ teaspoon salt.
½ teaspoon cinnamon.
½ teaspoon allspice.

½ nutmeg grated.

Follow directions for mixing butter cake mixtures.

Rich Coffee Cake.

1 cup butter.
2 cups sugar.
4 eggs.
2 tablespoons molasses.
1 cup cold boiled coffee.
3¾ cups flour.
5 teaspoons baking powder.
1 teaspoon cinnamon.

½ teaspoon clove.
½ teaspoon mace.
½ teaspoon allspice.
¾ cup raisins seeded and
 cut in pieces.
¾ cup currants.
¼ cup citron thinly sliced
 and cut in strips.

2 tablespoons brandy.

Follow directions for mixing butter cake mixtures. Bake in deep cake pans.

Dark Fruit Cake.

½ cup butter.
¾ cup brown sugar.
¾ cup raisins seeded and
   cut in pieces.
¾ cup currants.
½ cup citron thinly sliced
   and cut in strips.
½ cup molasses.

2 eggs.
½ cup milk.
2 cups flour.
½ teaspoon soda.
1 teaspoon cinnamon.
½ teaspoon allspice.
¼ teaspoon mace.
¼ teaspoon clove.

½ teaspoon lemon extract.

Follow directions for mixing butter cake mixtures.
Bake in deep cake pans one and one-quarter hours.

Nut Cakes.

Meat from 1 lb. pecans.
1 lb. powdered sugar.

¼ cup flour.
Whites 6 eggs.

1 teaspoon vanilla.

Pound nut meat and mix with sugar and flour. Beat
whites of eggs until stiff, add first mixture and vanilla.
Drop from tip of tablespoon (allowing one spoonful for
each drop) on a tin sheet covered with buttered paper.
Bake twenty minutes in a moderate oven.

Snow Cake.

¼ cup butter.
1 cup sugar.
½ cup milk.
1⅔ cups flour.

2½ teaspoons baking powder.
Whites 2 eggs.
½ teaspoon vanilla or
¼ teaspoon almond extract.

Follow recipe for mixing butter cakes. Bake forty-
five minutes in a deep narrow pan.

Lily Cake.

⅓ cup butter.
1 cup sugar.
½ cup milk.
1¾ cups flour.

2½ teaspoons baking powder.
Whites 3 eggs.
⅓ teaspoon lemon extract.
⅔ teaspoon vanilla.

Follow recipe for mixing butter cakes.

Corn-starch Cake.

1 cup butter.	4½ teaspoons baking powder.
2 cups sugar.	Whites 5 eggs.
1 cup milk.	¾ teaspoon vanilla or
1 cup corn-starch.	½ teaspoon almond extract.
2 cups flour.	

Follow recipe for mixing butter cakes. This mixture makes two loaves.

Prune Almond Cake.

Bake one-half Corn-starch Cake mixture in a dripping-pan. Cut in two crosswise, spread between layers Prune Almond Filling, and cover top with White Mountain Cream.

Prune Almond Filling. To one-half the recipe for White Mountain Cream add eight soft prunes stoned and cut in pieces, and one-fourth cup almonds blanched and cut in pieces.

Marshmallow Cake.

½ cup butter.	3 teaspoons baking powder.
1½ cups sugar.	¼ teaspoon cream of tartar.
½ cup milk.	Whites 5 eggs.
2 cups flour.	1 teaspoon vanilla.

Follow recipe for mixing butter cakes. Bake in shallow pans, and put Marshmallow Cream between the layers and on the top.

Fig Éclair.

½ cup butter (scant).	1⅞ cups flour.
1 cup sugar.	3 teaspoons baking powder.
½ cup milk.	Whites 4 eggs.
½ teaspoon vanilla.	

Follow recipe for mixing butter cakes. Bake in shallow pans, put between layers Fig Filling, and sprinkle top with powdered sugar.

Banana Cake.

Mix and bake Fig Éclair mixture; put between layers White Mountain Cream covered with thin slices of banana, and frost the top. This should be eaten the day it is made.

Bride's Cake.

½ cup butter.	3 teaspoons baking powder.
1½ cups sugar.	¼ teaspoon cream of tartar.
½ cup milk.	Whites six eggs.
2½ cups flour.	½ teaspoon almond extract.

Follow recipe for mixing butter cakes. Bake forty-five to fifty minutes in deep, narrow pans. Cover with white frosting.

Light Fruit Cake.

To Fig Éclair mixture add one-half cup raisins seeded and cut in pieces, two ounces citron thinly sliced and cut in strips, and one-third cup walnut meat cut in pieces. In making mixture, reserve one tablespoon flour to use for dredging fruit.

White Nut Cake.

¾ cup butter.	½ teaspoon cream of tartar.
1½ cups sugar.	3 teaspoons baking powder.
½ cup milk.	Whites 8 eggs.
2½ cups flour.	1 cup walnut meat cut in pieces.

Follow recipe for mixing butter cakes. This mixture makes two loaves.

Golden Cake.

¼ cup butter.	¼ cup milk.
½ cup sugar.	⅞ cup flour.
Yolks 5 eggs.	1½ teaspoons baking powder.

1 teaspoon orange extract.

Cream the butter, add sugar gradually, and yolks of eggs beaten until thick and lemon colored, and extract.

Mix and sift flour and baking powder, and add alternately with milk to first mixture. Omit orange extract, add one-half cup nut meat cut in small pieces, and bake in individual tins.

Mocha Cake.

Bake a sponge cake mixture in sheets. Shape in small rounds, and cut in three layers. Put layers together with a thin coating of frosting. Spread frosting around sides and roll in shredded cocoanut. Ornament top with frosting forced through a pastry bag and tube, using the rose tube. Begin at centre of top and coil frosting around until surface is covered. Garnish centre of top with a candied cherry.

Frosting. Wash one-third cup butter, add one cup powdered sugar gradually, and beat until creamy. Then add one cup Cream Filling which has been cooled. Flavor with one-half teaspoon vanilla and one and one-half squares melted chocolate.

This frosting is sometimes colored pink, yellow, green, or lavender, and flavored with rose, vanilla, or a combination of almond and vanilla. Large Mocha Cakes are baked in two round layer cake tins, each cake being cut in two layers. Layers are put together as small cakes. The top is spread smoothly with frosting, then ornamented with large pieces of candied fruits arranged in a design, and frosting forced through pastry bag and tube.

Cream Cakes.

½ cup butter.   4 eggs.
1 cup boiling water.   1 cup flour.

Put butter and water in saucepan and place on front of range. As soon as boiling point is reached, add flour all at once, and stir vigorously. Remove from fire as soon as mixed, and add unbeaten eggs one at a time, beating, until thoroughly mixed, between the addition of eggs. Drop by spoonfuls on a buttered sheet, one and one-half inches apart, shaping with handle of spoon as nearly cir-

cular as possible, having mixture slightly piled in centre.
Bake thirty minutes in a moderate oven.   With a sharp
knife make a cut in each large enough to admit of Cream
Filling.   This recipe makes eighteen small cream cakes.
For flavoring cream filling use lemon extract.   If cream
cakes are removed from oven before being thoroughly
cooked, they will fall.   If in doubt, take one from oven,
and if it does not fall, this is sufficient proof that others
are cooked.

French Cream Cakes.

Fill Cream Cakes with Cream Sauce I.

French Strawberry Cream Cakes.

Shape cream cake mixture oblong, making twelve
cakes.   Split and fill with Strawberry Cream Filling.

Éclairs.

Shape cream cake mixture four and one-half inches
long by one inch wide, by forcing through a pastry bag
and tube.   Bake twenty-five minutes in a moderate oven.
Split and fill with vanilla, coffee, or chocolate cream
filling.   Frost with Confectioners' Frosting to which is
added one-third cup melted Fondant, dipping top of
éclairs in frosting while it is hot.

Lemon Queens.

¼ lb. butter.	Yolks 4 eggs.
½ lb. sugar.	5 oz. flour.
Grated rind 1 lemon.	¼ teaspoon salt.
¾ tablespoon lemon juice.	¼ teaspoon soda.
Whites 4 eggs.	

Cream the butter, add sugar gradually, and continue
beating.   Then add grated rind, lemon juice, and yolks of
eggs beaten until thick and lemon colored.   Mix and sift
soda, salt, and flour; add to first mixture and beat thoroughly.   Add whites of eggs beaten stiff.   Bake from
twenty to twenty-five minutes in small tins.

Queen Cake.

⅔ cup butter.   Whites 6 eggs.
2 cups flour (scant).   1¼ cups powdered sugar.
¼ teaspoon soda.   1½ teaspoons lemon juice.

Cream the butter, add flour gradually, mixed and sifted with soda, then add lemon juice. Beat whites of eggs until stiff; add sugar gradually, and combine the mixtures. Bake fifty minutes in a long shallow pan. Cover with Opera Caramel Frosting.

Pound Cake.

1 lb. butter.   Whites 10 eggs.
1 lb. sugar.   1 lb. flour.
Yolks 10 eggs.   ½ teaspoon mace.
2 tablespoons brandy.

Cream the butter, add sugar gradually, and continue beating; then add yolks of eggs beaten until thick and lemon colored, whites of eggs beaten until stiff and dry, flour, mace, and brandy. Beat vigorously five minutes. Bake in a deep pan one and one fourth hours in a slow oven; or if to be used for fancy ornamented cakes, bake thirty to thirty-five minutes in a dripping-pan.

English Fruit Cake.

1 lb. butter.   2 tablespoons milk.
1 lb. light brown sugar.   3 lbs. currants.
9 eggs.   2 lbs. raisins seeded and
1 lb. flour.   finely chopped.
2 teaspoons mace.   ½ lb. almonds blanched and
2 teaspoons cinnamon,   shredded.
1 teaspoon soda.   1 lb. citron thinly sliced and
         cut in strips.

Cream the butter, add sugar gradually, and beat thoroughly. Separate yolks from whites of eggs; beat yolks until thick and lemon colored, whites until stiff and dry, and add to first mixture. Then add milk, fruit, and flour mixed and sifted with mace, cinnamon, and soda.

Put in deep pans, cover with buttered paper, steam three hours, and bake one and one-half hours in a slow oven, or bake four hours in a very slow oven.

Imperial Cake.

½ lb. butter.
½ lb. sugar.
Yolks 5 eggs.
Whites 5 eggs.
Grated rind ½ lemon.
2 teaspoons lemon juice.

½ lb. raisins seeded and cut in pieces.
½ cup walnut meat broken in pieces.
½ lb. flour.
¼ teaspoon soda.

Mix same as Pound Cake, adding raisins dredged with flour, and nuts at the last.

Wedding Cake.

1 lb. butter.
1 lb. sugar.
12 eggs.
1 lb. flour.
2 teaspoons cinnamon.
Nutmeg,
Allspice, } ¾ teaspoon
Mace, } each.

½ teaspoon clove.
3 lbs. raisins seeded and cut in pieces.
1 lb. currants.
1 lb. citron thinly sliced and cut in strips.
1 lb. figs finely chopped.
¼ cup brandy.

2 tablespoons lemon juice.

Cream the butter, add sugar gradually, and beat thoroughly. Separate yolks from whites of eggs; beat yolks until thick and lemon colored, whites until stiff and dry, and add to first mixture. Add flour (excepting one-third cup, which should be reserved to dredge fruit) mixed and sifted, with spices, brandy, and lemon juice. Then add fruit, except citron, dredged with reserved flour. Dredge citron with flour and put in layers between cake mixture when putting in the pan. Bake same as English Fruit Cake.

CHAPTER XI.

CAKE FILLINGS AND FROSTINGS.

Cream Filling.

⅞ cup sugar.   2 eggs.
⅓ cup flour.   2 cups scalded milk.
⅛ teaspoon salt.   1 teaspoon vanilla or
                               ½ teaspoon lemon extract.

Mix dry ingredients, add eggs slightly beaten, and pour on gradually scalded milk.   Cook fifteen minutes in double boiler, stirring constantly until thickened, afterwards occasionally.   Cool slightly and flavor.

Chocolate Cream Filling.

Put one and one-fourth squares Baker's chocolate in a saucepan and melt over hot water.   Add to Cream Filling, using in making one cup sugar in place of seven-eighths cup.

Coffee Cream Filling.

Flavor Cream Filling with one and one-half tablespoons coffee extract.

French Cream Filling.

¾ cup thick cream   ¼ cup powdered sugar.
¼ cup milk.   White one egg.
                 ½ teaspoon vanilla.

Dilute cream with milk and beat until stiff, using Dover egg-beater.   Add sugar, white of egg beaten until stiff, and vanilla.

Strawberry Filling.

1 cup thick cream.	White 1 egg.
⅓ cup sugar.	½ cup strawberries.
¼ teaspoon vanilla.	

Beat cream until stiff, using Dover egg-beater, add sugar, white of egg beaten until stiff, strawberries mashed, and vanilla.

Lemon Filling.

1 cup sugar.	¼ cup lemon juice.
2½ tablespoons flour.	1 egg.
Grated rind 2 lemons.	1 teaspoon butter.

Mix sugar and flour, add grated rind, lemon juice, and egg slightly beaten. Put butter in saucepan; when melted, add mixture, and stir constantly until boiling point is reached. Care must be taken that mixture does not adhere to bottom of saucepan. Cool before spreading.

Orange Filling.

½ cup sugar.	¼ cup orange juice.
2½ tablespoons flour.	½ tablespoon lemon juice.
Grated rind ½ orange.	1 egg slightly beaten.
1 teaspoon butter.	

Mix ingredients in order given. Cook ten minutes in double boiler, stirring constantly. Cool before spreading.

Chocolate Filling.

2½ squares chocolate.	3 tablespoons milk.
1 cup powdered sugar.	Yolk 1 egg.
½ teaspoon vanilla.	

Melt chocolate over hot water, add one-half the sugar, and milk; add remaining sugar, and yolk of egg; then cook in double boiler until it thickens, stirring constantly at first, that mixture may be perfectly smooth. Cool slightly, flavor, and spread.

Nut or Fruit Filling.

To White Mountain Cream add chopped walnuts, almonds, figs, dates, or raisins, separately or in combination.

Cocoanut Filling.

Whites 2 eggs.   Fresh grated cocoanut.
                  Powdered sugar.

Beat whites of eggs on a platter with a fork until stiff.
Add enough powdered sugar to spread. Spread over
cake, sprinkle thickly with cocoanut. Use for layer cake,
having filling between and on top.

Lemon Cocoanut Cream.

Juice and grated rind 1 lemon.   Yolks 2 eggs.
1 cup sugar.   1 cup shredded cocoanut.

Mix lemon juice and rind with sugar and yolks of eggs
slightly beaten; cook ten minutes in double boiler, stirring constantly; then add cocoanut. Cool and use as a
filling for Corn-starch Cake.

Fig Filling.

½ lb. figs finely chopped.   ⅓ cup boiling water.
⅓ cup sugar.   1 tablespoon lemon juice.

Mix ingredients in the order given and cook in double
boiler until thick enough to spread.

Marshmallow Paste.

¾ cup sugar.   ¼ lb. marshmallows.
¼ cup milk.   2 tablespoons hot water.
                  ½ teaspoon vanilla.

Put sugar and milk in a saucepan, heat slowly to boiling point without stirring, and boil six minutes. Break
marshmallows in pieces and melt in double boiler, add hot
water and cook until mixture is smooth, then add hot
syrup gradually, stirring constantly. Beat until cool
enough to spread, then add vanilla. This may be used
for both filling and frosting.

Pistachio Paste.

To Marshmallow Paste add a few drops extract of almond, one-third cup pistachio nuts blanched and chopped,
and leaf green to color. Use same as Marshmallow Paste.

Prune Almond Filling.

To White Mountain Cream add one-half cup selected prunes, stoned and cut in pieces, and one-third cup almonds blanched and chopped.

Confectioners' Frosting.

2 tablespoons boiling water. Confectioners' sugar.
Flavoring.

To water add enough sifted sugar to make of right consistency to spread; then add flavoring. Fresh fruit juice may be used in place of boiling water. This is a most satisfactory frosting, and is both easily and quickly made.

Orange Frosting.

Grated rind 1 orange. 1 tablespoon orange juice.
1 teaspoon brandy. Yolk 1 egg.
½ teaspoon lemon juice. Confectioners' sugar.

Add rind to brandy and fruit juices; let stand fifteen minutes. Strain, and add gradually to yolk of egg slightly beaten. Stir in confectioners' sugar until of right consistency to spread.

Gelatine Frosting.

2½ tablespoons boiling water. ¾ cup confectioners'
½ teaspoon granulated gelatine. sugar.
½ teaspoon vanilla.

Dissolve gelatine in boiling water. Add sugar and flavoring and beat until of right consistency to spread. Crease in squares when slightly hardened.

Plain Frosting.

White 1 egg. ½ teaspoon vanilla or
2 teaspoons cold water. ½ tablespoon lemon juice.
¾ cup confectioners' sugar.

Beat white of egg until stiff; add water and sugar. Beat thoroughly, then add flavoring. Use more sugar if needed. Spread with a broad-bladed knife.

Chocolate Frosting.

1½ squares chocolate.   Yolk 1 egg.
⅓ cup scalded cream.   ½ teaspoon melted butter.
Few grains salt.   Confectioners' sugar.
                ½ teaspoon vanilla.

Melt chocolate over hot water, add cream gradually, salt, yolk of egg, and butter. Stir in confectioners' sugar until of right consistency to spread; then add flavoring.

White Mountain Cream.

1 cup sugar.   1 teaspoon vanilla or
⅓ cup boiling water.   ½ tablespoon lemon juice.
White 1 egg.

Put sugar and water in saucepan, and stir to prevent sugar from adhering to saucepan; heat gradually to boiling point, and boil without stirring until syrup will thread when dropped from tip of spoon or tines of silver folk. Pour syrup gradually on beaten white of egg, beating mixture constantly, and continue beating until of right consistency to spread; then add flavoring and pour over cake, spreading evenly with back of spoon. Crease as soon as firm. If not beaten long enough, frosting will run; if beaten too long, it will not be smooth. Frosting beaten too long may be improved by adding a few drops of lemon juice or boiling water. This frosting is soft inside, and has a glossy surface. If frosting is to be ornamented with nuts or candied cherries, place them on frosting as soon as spread.

Boiled Frosting.

1 cup sugar.   1 teaspoon vanilla or
½ cup water.   ½ tablespoon lemon juice.
Whites 2 eggs.

Make same as White Mountain Cream. This frosting, on account of the larger quantity of egg, does not stiffen so quickly as White Mountain Cream, therefore is more successfully made by the inexperienced.

Boiled Chocolate Frosting.

To White Mountain Cream or Boiled Frosting add one and one-half squares melted chocolate as soon as syrup is added to whites of eggs.

Brown Frosting.

Make same as Boiled Frosting, using brown sugar in place of white sugar.

Maple Sugar Frosting.

1 lb. soft maple sugar.	½ cup boiling water.

Whites 2 eggs.

Break sugar in small pieces, put in saucepan with boiling water, and stir occasionally until sugar is dissolved. Boil without stirring until syrup will thread when dropped from tip of spoon. Pour syrup gradually on beaten whites, beating mixture constantly, and continue beating until of right consistency to spread.

Cream Maple Sugar Frosting.

1 lb. soft maple sugar.	1 cup cream.

Break sugar in small pieces, put in saucepan with cream, and stir occasionally until sugar is dissolved. Boil without stirring until a ball can be formed when mixture is tried in cold water. Beat until of right consistency to spread.

Milk Frosting.

1½ cups sugar.	1 teaspoon butter.
½ cup milk.	½ teaspoon vanilla.

Put butter in saucepan; when melted, add sugar and milk. Stir to be sure that sugar does not adhere to saucepan, heat to boiling point, and boil without stirring thirteen minutes. Remove from fire, and beat until of right consistency to spread; then add flavoring and pour over cake, spreading evenly with back of spoon. Crease as soon as firm.

Caramel Frosting.

Make as Milk Frosting, adding one and one-half squares melted chocolate as soon as boiling point is reached.

Opera Caramel Frosting.

1½ cups brown sugar.   ¾ cup thin cream.
½ tablespoon butter.

Boil ingredients together until a ball can be formed when mixture is tried in cold water. It takes about forty minutes for boiling. Beat until of right consistency to spread.

Fondant Icing.

The mixture in which small cakes are dipped for icing is fondant, the recipe for which may be found in chapter on Confections. Cakes for dipping must first be glazed.

To Glaze Cakes. Beat white of one egg slightly, and add one tablespoon powdered sugar. Apply with a brush to top and sides of cakes. After glazing, cakes should stand over night before dipping.

To Dip Cakes. Melt fondant over hot water, and color and flavor as desired. Stir to prevent crust from forming on top. Take cake to be dipped on a three-tined fork and lower in fondant three-fourths the depth of cake. Remove from fondant, invert, and slip from fork to a board. Decorate with ornamental frosting and nut meat, candied cherries, angelica, or candied violets. For small ornamented cakes, pound cake mixture is baked a little more than one inch thick in shallow pans, and when cool cut in squares, diamonds, triangles, circles, crescents, etc.

Ornamental Frosting I.

2 cups sugar.   Whites 3 eggs.
1 cup water.   ¼ teaspoon tartaric acid.

Boil sugar and water until syrup when dropped from tip of spoon forms a long thread. Pour syrup gradually on beaten whites of eggs, beating constantly; then add acid and continue beating. When stiff enough to spread, put a thin coating over cake. Beat remaining frosting until cold and stiff enough to keep in shape after being forced through a pastry tube. After first coating on cake has hardened, cover with a thicker layer, and crease for cutting. If frosting is too stiff to spread smoothly, thin with a few drops of water. With a pastry bag and variety of tubes, cake may be ornamented as desired.

Cake being ornamented with Ornamental Frosting.

Ornamental Frosting II.

Whites 3 eggs.   1 tablespoon lemon juice.
Confectioners' sugar, sifted.

Put eggs in a large bowl, add two tablespoons sugar, and beat three minutes, using a perforated wooden spoon. Repeat until one and one-half cups sugar are used. Add lemon juice gradually, as mixture thickens. Continue adding sugar by spoonfuls, and beating until frosting is stiff enough to spread. This may be determined by taking up some of mixture on back of spoon, and with a case knife making a cut through mixture; if knife makes a clean cut and frosting remains parted, it is of right consistency. Spread cake thinly with frosting; when this has hardened, put on a thicker layer, having mixture somewhat stiffer than first coating, and then crease for cutting. To remaining frosting add enough more sugar, that frosting may keep in shape after being forced through a pastry bag and tube.

With a pastry bag and variety of tubes, cake may be ornamented as desired.

CHAPTER XII.

FANCY CAKES AND CONFECTIONS.

A LMOND paste for making macaroons and small
fancy cakes may be bought of dealers who keep
confectioners' supplies, although sometimes a resident
baker or confectioner will sell a small quantity. Almond
paste is put up in five-pound tin pails, and retails for one
and one-half dollars per pail. During the cold weather
it will keep after being opened for a long time.

Macaroons.

½ lb. almond paste.   Whites 3 eggs.
⅜ lb. powdered sugar.

Work together almond paste and sugar on a smooth
board or marble slab. Then add whites of eggs
gradually, and work until mixture is perfectly smooth.
Confectioners at first use the hand, afterward a palette
knife, which is not only of use for mixing but for keeping
board clean. Shape, using a pastry bag and tube,
on a tin sheet covered with buttered paper, one-half
inch apart; or drop mixture from tip of spoon in small
piles. Macaroon mixture is stiff enough to hold its
shape, but in baking spreads. Bake fifteen to twenty
minutes in a slow oven. If liked soft, they should be
slightly baked. After removing from oven, invert paper,
and wet with a cloth wrung out of cold water, when
macaroons will easily slip off.

Almond Macaroons.

Sprinkle Macaroons, before baking, with almonds blanched and shredded, or chopped.

Crescents.

¼ lb. almond paste.   Almonds blanched and
2 oz. confectioners' sugar.   finely chopped.
White 1 small egg.

Mix same as Macaroons. Shape mixture, which is quite soft, in a long roll. Cut pieces from roll three-fourths inch long. Roll each separately in chopped nuts, at the same time shaping to form a crescent. Bake twenty minutes on a buttered tin sheet in a slow oven. Cool and frost with Confectioners' Frosting, made thin enough to apply with a brush, and flavored with lemon juice until quite acid. Other nuts may be used in place of almonds.

Cinnamon Bars.

10 oz. almond paste.   White 1 egg.
5 oz. confectioners' sugar.   ½ teaspoon cinnamon.

Mix same as Macaroons. Dredge a board with sugar, knead mixture slightly, and shape in a long roll. Pat and roll one-fourth inch thick, using a rolling-pin. After rolling, the piece should be four inches wide. Spread with frosting made of white of one egg and two-thirds cup confectioners' sugar beaten together until stiff enough to spread. Cut in strips four inches long by three-fourths inch wide. This must be quickly done, as a crust soon forms over frosting. To accomplish this, use two knives, one placed through mixture where dividing line is to be made, and the other used to make a clean sharp cut on both sides of first knife. Knives should be kept clean by wiping on a damp cloth. Remove strips, as soon as cut, to a tin sheet, greased with lard and then floured. Bake twenty minutes on centre grate in a slow oven.

Horseshoes.

Use Cinnamon Bar mixture. Cover with frosting colored with fruit red. Cut in strips six inches long by one-half inch wide. As soon as cut, shape quickly, at the same time carefully, in form of horseshoes. Bake same as Cinnamon Bars. When cool, make eight dots with chocolate frosting to represent naiis.

Cocoanut Cakes I.

½ lb. fresh grated cocoanut.   6 oz. sugar and glucose,
Whites 1½ eggs.   using one mixing-spoon
                                              glucose.

German Confectioner.

Cook cocoanut, sugar and glucose, in double boiler until mixture clings to spoon, add whites of eggs, stir vigorously, and cook until mixture feels sticky when tried between the fingers. Spread in a wet pan, cover with wet paper, and chill on ice. Shape in small balls, first dipping hands in cold water. Bake twenty minutes in a slow oven on a tin sheet greased with white wax.

Cocoanut Cakes II.

1 lb. fresh grated cocoanut.   ¾ lb. sugar.
Whites 2 eggs.

Cook, shape, and bake same as Cocoanut Cakes I.

Stuffed Dates I.

Make a cut the entire length of dates and remove stones. Fill cavities with castanea nuts, English walnuts, or blanched almonds, and shape in original form. Roll in granulated sugar. Pile in rows on a small plate covered with a doily. If castanea nuts are used, with a sharp knife cut off the brown skin which lies next to shell.

Stuffed Dates II.

Remove stones from dates and fill cavities with Neufchatel cheese.

Salted Almonds I.

Blanch one-fourth pound Jordan almonds and dry on a towel. Put one-third cup olive oil in a very small saucepan. When hot, put in one-fourth of the almonds and fry until delicately browned, stirring to keep almonds constantly in motion. Remove with a spoon or small skimmer, taking up as little oil as possible. Drain on brown paper and sprinkle with salt; repeat until all are fried. It may be necessary to remove some of the salt by wiping nuts with a napkin.

Salted Almonds II.

Prepare almonds as for Salted Almonds I. Fry in one-third cup fat, using half lard and half clarified butter or all cocoanut butter. Drain and sprinkle with salt.

Salted Peanuts.

In buying peanuts for salting, get those which have not been roasted. Remove skins and fry same as Salted Almonds I. or II.

Salted Pecans.

Shelled pecans may be bought by the pound, which is much the best way when used for salting, as it is difficult to remove the nut meat without breaking. Fry same as Salted Almonds I. or II. Care must be taken that they do not remain in fat too long; having a dark skin, color does not determine when they are sufficiently cooked.

Parisian Sweets.

1 lb. figs.	1 lb. English walnut meat.
1 lb. dates.	Confectioners' sugar.

Pick over and remove stems from figs and stones from dates. Mix fruit with walnut meat, and force through a meat-chopper. Work, using the hands, on a board dredged with confectioners' sugar, until well blended. Roll to one-fourth inch thickness, using confectioners' sugar for dredging board and pin. Shape with a small round cutter, first dipped in sugar, or cut with a sharp knife in three-fourth inch squares. Roll each piece in confectioners' sugar, and shake to remove superfluous sugar. Pack in layers in a tin box, putting paper between each layer. These confections may be used at dinner in place of bonbons or ginger chips. A combination of nut meat (walnut, almond, and filbert) may be used in equal proportions.

Molasses Candy.

2 cups Porto Rico molasses.	3 tablespoons butter.
⅔ cup sugar.	1 tablespoon vinegar.

An iron kettle with a rounding bottom (Scotch kettle), or copper kettle is best for candy making. If one has no copper kettle, a granite kettle is best for sugar candies.

Put butter in kettle, place over fire, and when melted, add molasses and sugar. Stir until sugar is dissolved. During the first of the boiling, stirring is unnecessary; but when nearly cooked, it should be constantly stirred. Boil until, when tried in cold water, mixture will become brittle. Add vinegar just before taking from fire. Pour into a well buttered pan. When cool enough to handle, pull until porous and light colored, allowing candy to come in contact with tips of fingers and thumbs, not to be squeezed in the hand. Cut in small pieces, using large shears or a sharp knife, and then arrange on slightly buttered plates to cool.

Velvet Molasses Candy.

1 cup molasses.	3 tablespoons vinegar.
3 cups sugar.	½ teaspoon cream of tartar.
1 cup boiling water.	½ cup melted butter.
¼ teaspoon soda.	

Put first four ingredients in kettle placed over front of range. As soon as boiling point is reached, add cream of tartar. Boil until, when tried in cold water, mixture will become brittle. Stir constantly during last part of cooking. When nearly done, add butter and soda. Pour into a buttered pan and pull same as Molasses Candy. While pulling, add one teaspoon vanilla, one-half teaspoon lemon extract, few drops oil of peppermint, or few drops oil of wintergreen.

Buttercups.

2 cups molasses.	2 tablespoons butter.
1 cup sugar.	⅓ teaspoon cream of tartar.
½ cup boiling water.	Fondant flavored with vanilla.

Boil ingredients (except fondant) until, when tried in cold water, a firm ball may be formed in the fingers, not stirring until the last few minutes of cooking. Pour on a buttered platter, and when cool enough to handle, pull until light colored. Shape on a floured board, having strip wide enough to enclose a roll of fondant one inch in diameter. Place fondant on candy, bring edges of candy together, and press firmly over fondant. With both hands pull candy into a long strip. Cut in small pieces; each piece will consist of fondant encircled with molasses candy. Care must be taken that candy is not cooked too long, as it should be soft rather than brittle.

Vinegar Candy.

2 cups sugar.	½ cup vinegar.
2 tablespoons butter.	

Put butter into kettle; when melted, add sugar and vinegar. Stir until sugar is dissolved, afterwards occasionally. Boil until, when tried in cold water, mixture will become brittle. Turn on a buttered platter to cool. Pull and cut same as Molasses Candy.

Ice Cream Candy.

3 cups sugar.	½ cup boiling water.
¼ teaspoon cream of tartar.	½ tablespoon vinegar.

Boil ingredients together without stirring, until, when tried in cold water, mixture will become brittle. Turn on a well buttered platter to cool. As edges cool, fold towards centre. As soon as it can be handled, pull until white and glossy. While pulling, flavor as desired, using vanilla, orange extract, coffee extract, oil of sassafras, or melted chocolate. Cut in sticks or small pieces.

Butter Scotch.

1 cup sugar.	2 tablespoons vinegar.
¼ cup molasses.	2 tablespoons boiling water.
	½ cup butter.

Boil ingredients together until, when tried in cold water, mixture will become brittle. Turn into a well buttered pan; when slightly cool, mark with a sharp-pointed knife in squares. This candy is much improved by cooking a small piece of vanilla bean with other ingredients.

Butter Taffy.

2 cups light brown sugar.	2 tablespoons water.
¼ cup molasses.	⅞ teaspoon salt.
2 tablespoons vinegar.	¼ cup butter.
	2 teaspoons vanilla.

Boil first five ingredients until, when tried in cold water, mixture will become brittle. When nearly done, add butter, and just before turning into pan, vanilla. Cool, and mark in squares.

Horehound Candy.

¾ square inch pressed horehound.	2 cups boiling water.
	3 cups sugar.
	½ teaspoon cream of tartar.

Pour boiling water over horehound which has been separated in pieces; let stand one minute, then strain through double cheese cloth. Put into a granite kettle with remaining ingredients, and boil until, when tried in cold water, mixture will become brittle. Turn into a buttered pan, cool slightly, then mark in small squares. Small square packages of horehound may be bought for five cents.

Chocolate Caramels.

2½ tablespoons butter.	½ cup milk.
2 cups molasses.	3 squares chocolate.
1 cup brown sugar.	1 teaspoon vanilla.

Put butter into kettle; when melted, add molasses, sugar, and milk. Stir until sugar is dissolved, and when boiling point is reached, add chocolate, stirring constantly until chocolate is melted. Boil until, when tried in cold water, a firm ball may be formed in the fingers. Add vanilla just after taking from fire. Turn into a buttered pan, cool, and mark in small squares.

Nut Chocolate Caramels.

To Chocolate Caramels add the meat from one pound English walnuts broken in pieces, or one-half pound almonds blanched and chopped.

Peanut Nougat.

1 lb. sugar.	1 quart peanuts.

Shell, remove skins, and finely chop peanuts. Sprinkle with one-fourth teaspoon salt. Put sugar in a perfectly smooth granite saucepan, place on range, and stir constantly until melted to a syrup, taking care to keep sugar from sides of pan. Add nut meat, pour at once into a warm buttered tin, and mark in small squares. If sugar is not removed from range as soon as melted, it will quickly caramelize.

Nut Bar.

Cover the bottom of a buttered shallow pan with one and one-third cups nut meat (castaneas, English walnuts, or almonds) cut in quarters. Pour over one pound sugar, melted as for Peanut Nougat. Mark in bars.

French Nougat.

½ lb. confectioners' sugar.   ¼ lb. almonds blanched
                                   and finely chopped.
Confectioners' chocolate.

Put sugar in a saucepan, place on range, and stir constantly until melted; add almonds, and pour on an oiled marble. Fold mixture as it spreads with a broad-bladed knife, keeping it constantly in motion. Divide in four parts, and as soon as cool enough to handle shape in long rolls about one-third inch in diameter, keeping rolls in motion until almost cold. When cold, snap in pieces one and one-half inches long. This is done by holding roll at point to be snapped over the sharp edge of a broad-bladed knife and snapping. Melt confectioners' chocolate over hot water, beat with a fork until light and smooth, and when slightly cooled dip pieces in chocolate and with a two-tined fork or bonbon dipper remove from chocolate to oiled paper, drawing dipper through top of each the entire length, thus leaving a ridge. Chocolate best adapted for dipping bonbons and confections must be bought where confectioners' supplies are kept.

Nougatine Drops.

Drop French Nougat mixture from the tip of a spoon on an oiled marble very soon after taking from fire. These drops have a rough surface. When cold, dip in melted confectioners' chocolate.

Wintergreen Wafers.

1 oz. gum tragacanth.   Confectioners' sugar.
1 cup cold water.   Oil of wintergreen.

Soak gum tragacanth in water twenty-four hours, and rub through a fine wire sieve; add enough confectioners' sugar to knead. Flavor with a few drops oil of wintergreen. If liked pink, color with fruit red. Roll until very thin on a board or marble dredged with sugar. Shape with a small round cutter or cut in three-fourths inch squares. Spread wafers, cover, and let stand until dry and brittle. This mixture may be flavored with oil of lemon, clove, sassafras, etc., and colored as desired.

Cocoanut Cream Candy.

1½ cups sugar. 2 teaspoons butter.
½ cup milk. ⅓ cup shredded cocoanut.
  ½ teaspoon vanilla.

Put butter into granite saucepan; when melted, add sugar and milk, and stir until sugar is dissolved. Heat to boiling point, and boil twelve minutes; remove from fire, add cocoanut and vanilla, and beat until creamy and mixture begins to sugar slightly around edge of saucepan. Pour at once into a buttered pan, cool slightly, and mark in squares. One-half cup nut meat, broken in pieces, may be used in place of cocoanut.

Chocolate Cream Candy.

2 cups sugar. 1 tablespoon butter.
⅔ cup milk. 2 squares chocolate.
  1 teaspoon vanilla.

Put butter into granite saucepan; when melted, add sugar and milk. Heat to boiling point; then add chocolate, and stir constantly until chocolate is melted. Boil thirteen minutes, remove from fire, add vanilla, and beat until creamy and mixture begins to sugar slightly around edge of saucepan. Pour at once into a buttered pan, cool slightly, and mark in squares. Omit vanilla, and add, while cooking, one-fourth teaspoon cinnamon.

Maple Sugar Candy.

1 lb. soft maple sugar. ¼ cup boiling water.
¾ cup thin cream. ⅔ cup English walnut or pecan
      meat cut in pieces.

Break sugar in pieces; put into a saucepan with cream and water. Bring to boiling point, and boil until a soft ball is formed when tried in cold water. Remove from fire, beat until creamy, add nut meat, and pour into a buttered tin. Cool slightly, and mark in squares.

Sultana Caramels.

2 cups sugar.	2 squares chocolate.
½ cup milk.	1 teaspoon vanilla.
¼ cup molasses.	½ cup English walnut or hickory
¼ cup butter.	nut meat cut in pieces.
2 tablespoons Sultana raisins.	

Put butter into a saucepan; when melted, add sugar, milk, and molasses. Heat to boiling point, and boil seven minutes. Add chocolate, and stir until chocolate is melted; then boil seven minutes longer. Remove from fire, beat until creamy, add nuts, raisins, and vanilla, and pour at once into a buttered tin. Cool slightly, and mark in squares.

Pralines.

1⅞ cups powdered sugar.	2 cups hickory nut or pecan
1 cup maple syrup.	meat cut in pieces.
½ cup cream.	

Boil first three ingredients until, when tried in cold water, a soft ball may be formed. Remove from fire, and beat until of a creamy consistency; add nuts, and drop from tip of spoon in small piles on buttered paper.

Creamed Walnuts.

White 1 egg.	¾ teaspoon vanilla.
½ tablespoon cold water.	1 lb. confectioners' sugar.
English walnuts.	

Put egg, water, and vanilla in a bowl, and beat until well blended. Add sugar gradually until stiff enough to knead. Shape in balls, flatten, and place halves of walnuts opposite each other on each piece. Sometimes all the sugar will not be required.

Peppermints.

1½ cups sugar.   ½ cup boiling water.
6 drops oil of peppermint.

Put sugar and water into a granite saucepan and stir
until sugar is dissolved.   Boil ten minutes; remove from
fire, add peppermint, and beat until of right consistency
Drop from tip of spoon on slightly buttered paper.

BOILED SUGAR FOR CONFECTIONS.

Eleven tests are considered for boiling sugar : —

Small thread,	215° F.	The feather,	232°.
Large thread,	217°.	Soft ball,	238°.
Pearl,	220°.	Hard ball,	248°.
Large pearl,	222°.	Small crack,	290°.
The blow,	230°.	Crack,	310°.

Caramel, 350°.

Fondant, the basis of all French candy, is made of
sugar and water boiled together (with a small quantity
of cream of tartar to prevent sugar from granulating) to
soft ball, 238° F.   The professional confectioner is able
to decide when syrup has boiled to the right temperature
by sound while boiling, and by testing in cold water;
these tests at first seem somewhat difficult to the amateur,
but only a little experience is necessary to make fondant
successfully.   A sugar thermometer is often employed,
and proves valuable, as by its use one need not exercise
his judgment.

White Fondant.

2½ lbs. sugar.   1½ cups hot water.
¼ teaspoon cream of tartar.

Put ingredients into a smooth granite stewpan.   Stir,
place on range, and heat gradually to boiling point.
Boil without stirring until, when tried in cold water, a
soft ball may be formed that will just keep in shape,
which is 238° F.   After a few minutes' boiling, sugar will

adhere to sides of kettle; this should be washed off with the hand first dipped in cold water. Have a pan of cold water near at hand, dip hand in cold water, then quickly wash off a small part of the sugar with tips of fingers, and repeat until all sugar adhering to side of saucepan is removed. If this is quickly done, there is no danger of burning the fingers. Pour slowly on a slightly oiled marble slab. Let stand a few minutes to cool, but not long enough to become hard around the edge. Scrape fondant with chopping knife to one end of marble, and work with a wooden spatula until white and creamy. It will quickly change from this consistency, and begin to lump, when it should be kneaded with the hands until perfectly smooth.

Put into a bowl, cover with oiled paper to exclude air, that a crust may not form on top, and let stand twenty-four hours. A large oiled platter and wooden spoon may be used in place of marble slab and spatula. Always make fondant on a clear day, as a damp, heavy atmosphere has an unfavorable effect on the boiling of sugar.

Coffee Fondant.

2½ lbs. sugar.	¼ cup ground coffee.
1½ cups cold water.	¼ teaspoon cream of tartar.

Put water and coffee in saucepan, and heat to boiling point. Strain through double cheese cloth; then add sugar and cream of tartar. Boil and work same as White Fondant.

Maple Fondant.

1¼ lbs. maple sugar.	1 cup hot water.
1¼ lbs. sugar.	¼ teaspoon cream of tartar.

Break maple sugar in pieces, and add to remaining ingredients. Boil and work same as White Fondant.

Bonbons.

The centres of bonbons are made of fondant shaped in small balls. If White Fondant is used, flavor as desired, — vanilla being usually preferred. For cocoanut centres, work as much shredded cocoanut as possible into a small quantity of fondant; for nut centres, surround pieces of nut meat with fondant, using just enough to cover. French candied cherries are often used in this way. Allow balls to stand over night, and dip the following day.

To Dip Bonbons. Put fondant in saucepan, and melt over hot water; color and flavor as desired. In coloring fondant, dip a small wooden skewer in coloring paste, take up a small quantity, and dip skewer in fondant. If care is not taken, the color is apt to be too intense. During dipping, keep fondant over hot water that it may be kept of right consistency. For dipping, use a two-tined fork or confectioners' bonbon dipper. Drop centres in fondant one at a time, stir until covered, remove from fondant, put on oiled paper, and bring end of dipper over the top of bonbon, thus leaving a tail-piece which shows that bonbons have been hand dipped. Stir fondant between dippings to prevent a crust from forming.

Cream Mints.

Melt fondant over hot water, flavor with a few drops of oil of peppermint, wintergreen, clove, cinnamon, or orange, and color if desired. Drop from tip of spoon on oiled paper. Confectioners use rubber moulds for shaping cream mints; but these are expensive for home use, unless one is to make mints in large quantities.

Cream Nut Bars.

Melt fondant and flavor, stir in any kind of nut meat, cut in pieces. Turn in an oiled pan, cool, and cut in bars with a sharp knife. Maple Fondant is delicious with nuts.

Dipped Walnuts.

Melt fondant and flavor. Dip halves of walnuts as bonbon centres are dipped. Halves of pecan or whole blanched almonds may be similarly dipped.

Tutti-Frutti Candy.

Fill an oiled border-mould with three layers of melted fondant. Have bottom layer maple, well mixed with English walnut meat; the second layer colored pink, flavored with rose, and mixed with candied cherries cut in quarters and figs finely chopped; the third layer white, flavored with vanilla, mixed with nuts, candied cherries cut in quarters, and candied pineapple cut in small pieces. Cover mould with oiled paper, and let stand over night. Remove from mould, and place on a plate covered with a lace paper napkin. Fill centre with Bonbons and Glacé Nuts.

Glacé Nuts.

2 cups sugar. 1 cup boiling water.
⅛ teaspoon cream of tartar.

Put ingredients in a smooth saucepan, stir, place on range, and heat to boiling point. Boil without stirring until syrup begins to discolor, which is 310° F. Wash off sugar which adheres to sides of saucepan as in making fondant. Remove saucepan from fire, and place in larger pan of cold water to instantly stop boiling. Remove from cold water and place in a saucepan of hot water during dipping. Take nuts separately on a long pin, dip in syrup to cover, remove from syrup, and place on oiled paper.

Glacé Fruits.

For Glacé Fruits, grapes, strawberries, sections of mandarins and oranges, and candied cherries are most commonly used. Take grapes separately from clusters, leaving a short stem on each grape. Dip in syrup made as for Glacé Nuts, holding by stem with pincers. Remove to oiled paper. Glacé fruits keep but a day, and should only be attempted in cold and clear weather.

Spun Sugar.

2 lbs. sugar.   2 cups boiling water.
¼ teaspoon cream of tartar.

Put ingredients in a smooth saucepan. Boil without stirring until syrup begins to discolor, which is 300° F. Wash off sugar which adheres to sides of saucepan as in making fondant. Remove saucepan from fire, and place in a larger pan of cold water to instantly stop boiling. Remove from cold water, and place in saucepan of hot water. Place two broomstick-handles over backs of chairs, and spread paper on the floor under them. When syrup is slightly cooled, put dipper in syrup, remove from syrup, and shake quickly back and forth over broom-handles. Carefully take off spun sugar as soon as formed, and shape in nests or pile lightly on a cold dish. Syrup may be colored if desired. Spun Sugar is served around bricks or moulds of frozen creams and ices.

Dippers for spinning sugar are made of coarse wires; about twenty wires, ten inches long, are put in a bundle, and fastened with wire coiled round and round to form a handle.

CHAPTER XIII.

COOKING, PRESERVING, AND CANNING FRUITS.

FRUITS are usually at their best when served ripe and in season; however, a few cannot be taken in their raw state, and still others are rendered more easy of digestion by cooking. The methods employed are stewing and baking. Fruit should be cooked in earthen or granite ware utensils, and silver or wooden spoons should be employed for stirring. It must be remembered that all fruits contain one or more acids, and when exposed to air and brought in contact with an iron or tin surface, a poisonous compound may be formed.

Baked Apples.

Wipe and core sour apples. Put in a baking-dish, and fill cavities with sugar and spice. Allow one-half cup sugar and one-fourth teaspoon cinnamon or nutmeg to eight apples. If nutmeg is used, a few drops lemon juice and few gratings from rind of lemon to each apple is an improvement. Cover bottom of dish with boiling water, and bake in a hot oven until soft, basting often with syrup in dish. Serve hot or cold with cream. Many prefer to pare apples before baking. When this is done, core before paring, that fruit may keep in shape. In the fall, when apples are at their best, do not add spices to apples, as their flavor cannot be improved; but towards spring they become somewhat tasteless, and spice is an improvement.

Baked Sweet Apples.

Wipe and core eight sweet apples. Put in a baking-dish, and fill cavities with sugar, allowing one-third cup, or sweeten with molasses. Add two-thirds cup boiling water. Cover, and bake three hours in a slow oven, adding more water if necessary.

Apple Sauce.

Wipe, quarter, core, and pare eight sour apples. Make a syrup by boiling seven minutes one cup sugar and one cup water with thin shaving from rind of a lemon. Remove lemon, add enough apples to cover bottom of sauce-pan, watch carefully during cooking, and remove as soon as soft. Continue until all are cooked. Strain remaining syrup over apples.

Spiced Apple Sauce.

Wipe, quarter, core, and pare eight sour apples. Put in a saucepan, sprinkle with one cup sugar, add eight cloves, and enough water to prevent apples from burning. Cook to a mush, stirring occasionally.

Apple Ginger.

Wipe, quarter, core, pare, and chop two and one-half pounds sour apples. Put in a stewpan and add one and one-half pounds light brown sugar, juice and rind of one and one-half lemons, one-half ounce ginger root, and enough water to prevent apples from burning. Cover, and cook slowly four hours, adding water as necessary. Apple Ginger may be kept for several weeks.

Apple Porcupine.

Make a syrup by boiling eight minutes one and one-half cups sugar and one and one-half cups water. Wipe, core, and pare eight apples. Put apples in syrup as soon as pared, that they may not discolor. Cook until soft, occasionally skimming syrup during cooking. Apples cook better covered with the syrup; therefore it is better to use a deep saucepan and have two cookings. Drain apples from syrup, cool, fill cavities with jelly, marmalade, or preserved fruit, and stick apples with almonds blanched and split in halves lengthwise. Serve with Cream Sauce I.

Baked Bananas.

Remove skins from six bananas and cut in halves lengthwise. Put in a shallow granite pan or on an old platter. Mix two tablespoons melted butter, one-third cup sugar, and two tablespoons lemon juice. Baste bananas with one-half the mixture. Bake twenty minutes in a slow oven, basting during baking with remaining mixture.

Sautéd Bananas.

Remove skins from bananas, cut in halves lengthwise, and again cut in halves crosswise. Dredge with flour, and sauté in clarified butter. Drain, and sprinkle with powdered sugar.

Baked Peaches.

Peel, cut in halves, and remove stones from six peaches. Place in a shallow granite pan. Fill each cavity with one teaspoon sugar, one-half teaspoon butter, few drops lemon juice, and a slight grating nutmeg. Cook twenty minutes, and serve on circular pieces of buttered dry toast.

Baked Pears.

Wipe, quarter, and core pears. Put in a deep pudding-dish, sprinkle with sugar or add a small quantity of molasses, then add water to prevent pears from burning. Cover, and cook two or three hours in a very slow oven. Small pears may be baked whole. Seckel pears are delicious when baked.

Baked Quinces.

Wipe, quarter, core, and pare eight quinces. Put in a baking-dish, sprinkle with three-fourths cup sugar, add one and one-half cups water, cover, and cook until soft in a slow oven. Quinces require a long time for cooking.

Cranberry Sauce.

Pick over and wash three cups cranberries. Put in a stewpan, add one and one-fourth cups sugar and one cup boiling water. Cover, and boil ten minutes. Care must be taken that they do not boil over. Skim and cool.

Cranberry Jelly.

Pick over and wash four cups cranberries. Put in a stewpan with one cup boiling water, and boil twenty minutes. Rub through a sieve, add two cups sugar, and cook five minutes. Turn into a mould or glasses.

Stewed Prunes.

Wash and pick over prunes. Put in a saucepan, cover with cold water, and soak two hours; then cook until soft in same water. When nearly cooked, add sugar or molasses to sweeten. Many prefer the addition of a small quantity of lemon juice.

Rhubarb Sauce.

Peel and cut rhubarb in one-inch pieces. Put in a saucepan, sprinkle generously with sugar, and add enough water to prevent rhubarb from burning. Rhubarb contains such a large percentage of water that but little additional water is needed. Cook until soft. If rhubarb is covered with boiling water, allowed to stand five minutes, then drained and cooked, less sugar will be required. Rhubarb is sometimes baked in an earthen pudding-dish. If baked slowly for a long time it has a rich red color.

JELLIES.

Jellies are made of cooked fruit juice and sugar, in nearly all cases the proportions being equal. Where failures occur, they may usually be traced to the use of too ripe fruit.

To Prepare Glasses for Jelly. Wash glasses, and put in a kettle of cold water; place on range, and heat water gradually to boiling point. Remove glasses, and drain. Place glasses while filling on a cloth wrung out of hot water.

To Cover Jelly Glasses. Cut letter paper in circular pieces to just fit in top of glasses. Dip in brandy, and cover jelly. Put on tin covers or circular pieces of paper cut larger than the glasses, and fastened securely over the edge with mucilage.

To Make a Jelly Bag. Fold two opposite corners of a piece of cotton and wool flannel three-fourths yard long. Sew up in the form of a cornucopia, rounding at the end. Fell the seam to make more secure. Bind the top with tape, and furnish with two or three heavy loops by which it may be hung.

Apple Jelly.

Wipe apples, remove stem and blossom ends, and cut in quarters. Put in a granite or porcelain-lined preserving kettle, and add cold water to come nearly to top of apples. Cover, and cook slowly until apples are soft; mash, and drain through a coarse sieve. Avoid squeezing apples, which makes jelly cloudy. Then allow juice to drip through a double thickness of cheese cloth or a jelly bag. Boil twenty minutes, and add an equal quantity of heated sugar; boil five minutes, skim, and turn in glasses. Put in a sunny window, and let stand twenty-four hours. Cover, and keep in a cool, dry place. Porter apples make a delicious flavored jelly. If apples are pared, a much lighter jelly may be made. Gravenstein apples make a very spicy jelly.

To Heat Sugar. Put in a granite dish, place in oven, leaving oven door ajar, and stir occasionally.

Quince Jelly.

Follow recipe for Apple Jelly, using quinces in place of apples, and removing seeds from fruit. Quince parings are often used for jelly, the better part of the fruit being used for canning.

Crab Apple Jelly.

Follow recipe for Apple Jelly, leaving apples whole instead of cutting in quarters.

Currant Jelly.

Currants are in the best condition for making jelly between June twenty-eighth and July third, and should not be picked directly after a rain. Cherry currants make the best jelly. Equal proportions of red and white currants are considered desirable, and make a lighter colored jelly.

Pick over currants, but do not remove stems; wash and drain. Mash a few in the bottom of a preserving kettle, using a wooden potato masher; so continue until berries are used. Cook slowly until currants look white. Strain through a coarse strainer, then allow juice to drop through a double thickness of cheese cloth or a jelly bag. Measure, bring to boiling point, and boil five minutes; add an equal measure of heated sugar, boil three minutes, skim, and pour into glasses. Place in a sunny window, and let stand twenty-four hours. Cover, and keep in a cool, dry place.

Currant and Raspberry Jelly.

Follow recipe for Currant Jelly, using equal parts of currants and raspberries.

Blackberry Jelly.

Follow recipe for Currant Jelly, using blackberries in place of currants.

Raspberry Jelly.

Follow recipe for Currant Jelly, using raspberries in place of currants. Raspberry Jelly is the most critical to make, and should not be attempted if fruit is thoroughly ripe, or if it has been long picked.

Barberry Jelly.

Barberry Jelly is firmer and of better color if made from fruit picked before the frost comes, while some of the berries are still green. Make same as Currant Jelly, allowing one cup water to one peck barberries.

Grape Jelly.

Grapes should be picked over, washed, and stems removed before putting into a preserving kettle. Heat to boiling point, mash, and boil thirty minutes; then proceed as for Currant Jelly. Wild grapes make the best jelly.

Green Grape Jelly.

Grapes should be picked when just beginning to turn. Make same as Grape Jelly.

Venison Jelly.

1 peck wild grapes.	Whole cloves, ⎱ ¼ cup
1 quart vinegar.	Stick cinnamon, ⎰ each.
6 pounds sugar.	

Put first four ingredients into a preserving kettle, heat slowly to the boiling point, and cook until grapes are soft. Strain through a double thickness of cheese cloth or a jelly bag, and boil liquid twenty minutes; then add sugar heated, and boil five minutes. Turn into glasses.

Damson Jelly.

Wipe and pick over damsons; then prick several times with a large pin. Make same as Currant Jelly, using three-fourths as much sugar as fruit juice.

JAMS.

Raspberries and blackberries are the fruits most often employed for making jams, and require equal weight of sugar and fruit.

Raspberry Jam.

Pick over raspberries. Mash a few in the bottom of a preserving kettle, using a wooden potato masher, and so continue until the fruit is used. Heat slowly to boiling point, and add gradually an equal quantity of heated sugar. Cook slowly forty-five minutes. Put in a stone jar or tumblers.

Blackberry Jam.

Follow recipe for Raspberry Jam, using blackberries in place of raspberries.

MARMALADES.

Marmalades are made of the pulp and juice of fruits with sugar.

Grape Marmalade.

Pick over, wash, drain, and remove stems from grapes. Separate pulp from skins. Put pulp in preserving kettle. Heat to boiling point, and cook slowly until seeds separate from pulp; then rub through a hair sieve. Return to kettle with skins, add an equal measure of sugar, and cook slowly thirty minutes, occasionally stirring to prevent burning. Put in a stone jar or tumblers.

Quince Marmalade.

Wipe quinces, remove blossom ends, cut in quarters, remove seeds; then cut in small pieces. Put into a preserving kettle, and add enough water to nearly cover.

Cook slowly until soft. Rub through a hair sieve, and add three-fourths its measure of heated sugar. Cook slowly twenty minutes, stirring occasionally to prevent burning. Put in tumblers.

Orange Marmalade.

Select sour, smooth-skinned oranges. Weigh oranges, and allow three-fourths their weight in cut sugar. Remove peel from oranges in quarters. Cook peel until soft in enough boiling water to cover; drain, remove white part from peel by scraping it with a spoon. Cut thin yellow rind in strips, using a pair of scissors. This is more quickly accomplished by cutting through two or three pieces at a time. Divide oranges in sections, remove seeds and tough part of skin. Put into a preserving kettle and heat to boiling point, add sugar gradually, and cook slowly one hour; add rind, and cook one hour longer. Turn into glasses.

Orange and Rhubarb Marmalade.

Remove peel in quarters from eight oranges and prepare as for Orange Marmalade. Divide oranges in sections, remove seeds and tough part of skin. Put into a preserving kettle, add five pounds rhubarb, skinned and cut in one-half inch pieces. Heat to boiling point, and boil one-half hour; then add four pounds cut sugar and cut rind. Cook slowly two hours. Turn into glasses.

CANNING AND PRESERVING.

Preserving fruit is cooking it with from three-fourths to its whole weight of sugar. By so doing, much of the natural flavor of the fruit is destroyed; therefore canning is usually preferred to preserving.

Canning fruit is preserving sterilized fruit in sterilized air-tight jars, the sugar being added to give sweetness. Fruits may be canned without sugar if perfectly sterilized, that is, freed from all germ life.

Directions for Canning.

Fruit for canning should be fresh, firm, of good quality, and not over-ripe. If over-ripe, some of the spores may survive the boiling, then fermentation will take place in a short time.

For canning fruit, allow one third its weight in sugar, and two and one-half to three cups water to each pound of sugar, Boil sugar and water ten minutes to make a thin syrup; then cook a small quantity of the fruit at a time in the syrup; by so doing, fruit may be kept in perfect shape. Hard fruits like pineapple and quince are cooked in boiling water until nearly soft, then put in syrup to finish cooking. Sterilized jars are then filled with fruit, and enough syrup added to overflow jars. If there is not sufficient syrup, add boiling water, as jars must be filled to overflow. Introduce a spoon between fruit and jar, that air bubbles may rise to the top and break; then quickly put on rubbers and screw on sterilized covers. Let stand until cold, again screw covers, being sure this time that jars are air tight. While filling jars place them on a cloth wrung out of hot water.

To Sterilize Jars.

Wash jars and fill with cold water. Set in a kettle on a trivet, and surround with cold water. Heat gradually to boiling point, remove from water, empty, and fill while hot. Put covers in hot water and let stand five minutes. Dip rubber bands in hot water, but do not allow them to stand. New rubbers should be used each season, and care must be taken that rims of covers are not bent, as jars cannot then be hermetically sealed.

Canned Porter Apples.

Wipe, quarter, core, and pare Porter apples, then weigh. Make a syrup by boiling for ten minutes one-third their weight in sugar with water, allowing two and one-half cups to each pound of sugar. Cook apples in syrup until soft, doing a few at a time. Fill jars, following Directions for Canning.

Canned Peaches.

Wipe peaches and put in boiling water, allowing them to stand just long enough to easily loosen skins. Remove skins and cook fruit at once, that it may not discolor, following Directions for Canning. Some prefer to pare peaches, sprinkle with sugar, and let stand over night. In morning drain, add water to fruit syrup, bring to boiling point, and then cook fruit. Peaches may be cut in halves, or smaller pieces if desired.

Canned Pears.

Wipe and pare fruit. Cook whole with stems left on, or remove stems, cut in quarters, and core. Follow Directions for Canning. A small piece of ginger root or a few slicings of lemon rind may be cooked with syrup. Bartlett pears are the best for canning.

Canned Pineapples.

Remove skin and eyes from pineapples; then cut in half-inch slices, and slices in cubes, at the same time discarding the core. Follow Directions for Canning. Pineapples may be shredded and cooked in one-half their weight of sugar without water, and then put in jars. When put up in this way they are useful for the making of sherbets and fancy desserts.

Canned Quinces.

Wipe, quarter, core, and pare quinces. Follow Directions for Canning. Quinces may be cooked with an equal weight of sweet apples; in this case use no extra sugar for apples.

Canned Cherries.

Use large white or red cherries. Wash, remove stems, then follow Directions for Canning.

Canned Huckleberries.

Pick over and wash berries, then put in a preserving kettle with a small quantity of water to prevent berries from burning. Cook until soft and put in jars. No sugar is required, but a sprinkling of salt is an agreeable addition.

Canned Rhubarb.

Pare rhubarb and cut in one-inch pieces. Pack in a jar, put under cold water faucet, and let water run twenty minutes, then screw on cover. Rhubarb canned in this way has often been known to keep a year.

Canned Tomatoes.

Wipe tomatoes, cover with boiling water, and let stand until skins may be easily removed. Cut in pieces and cook until thoroughly scalded; skim often during cooking. Fill jars, following directions given.

Damson Preserves.

Wipe damsons, and prick each fruit five or six times, using a large needle; then weigh. Make a syrup by boiling three-fourths their weight in sugar with water, allowing one cup to each pound of sugar. As soon as syrup reaches boiling point, skim, and add plums, a few at a time, that fruit may better keep in shape during cooking. Cook until soft. It is well to use two kettles, that work may be more quickly done, and syrup need not cook too long a time. Put into glass or stone jars.

Strawberry Preserves.

Pick over, wash, drain, and hull strawberries; then weigh. Fill jars with berries. Make a syrup same as for Damson Preserve, cooking syrup fifteen minutes. Add syrup to fruit to overflow jars; let stand fifteen minutes, when fruit will have shrunk, and more fruit must be added to fill jars. Screw on covers, put in a kettle of cold water, heat water to boiling point, and keep just below boiling point one hour.

Raspberries may be preserved in the same way.

Pear Chips.

8 lbs. pears.	¼ lb. Canton ginger.
4 lbs. sugar.	4 lemons.

Wipe pears, remove stems, quarter, and core; then cut in small pieces. Add sugar and ginger, and let stand over night. In the morning add lemons cut in small pieces, rejecting seeds, and cook slowly three hours. Put into a stone jar.

Raspberry and Currant Preserve.

6 lbs. currants.	6 lbs. sugar.
	8 quarts raspberries.

Pick over, wash, and drain currants. Put into a preserving kettle, adding a few at a time, and mash. Cook one hour, strain through double thickness of cheese cloth. Return to kettle, add sugar, heat to boiling point, and cook slowly twenty minutes. Add one quart raspberries when syrup again reaches boiling point, skim out raspberries, put in jar, and repeat until raspberries are used. Fill jars to overflowing with syrup, and screw on tops.

Brandied Peaches.

1 peck peaches.	Half their weight in sugar.
	1 quart high-proof alcohol or brandy.

Remove skins from peaches, and put alternate layers of peaches and sugar in a stone jar; then add alcohol. Cover closely, having a heavy piece of cloth under cover of jar.

Tutti-Frutti.

Put one pint brandy into a stone jar, add the various fruits as they come into market; to each quart of fruit add the same quantity of sugar, and stir the mixture each morning until all the fruit has been added. Raspberries, strawberries, apricots, peaches, cherries, and pineapples are the best to use.

Preserved Melon Rind.

Pare and cut in strips the rind of ripe melons. Soak in alum water to cover, allowing two teaspoons powdered alum to each quart of water. Heat gradually to boiling point and cook slowly ten minutes. Drain, cover with ice water, and let stand two hours; again drain, and dry between towels. Weigh, allow one pound sugar to each pound of fruit, and one cup water to each pound of sugar. Boil sugar and water ten minutes. Add melon rind, and cook until tender. Remove rind to a stone jar, and cover with syrup. Two lemons cut in slices may be cooked ten minutes in the syrup.

Tomato Preserve.

1 lb. yellow pear tomatoes.	2 oz. preserved Canton ginger.
1 lb. sugar.	2 lemons.

Peel tomatoes, cover with sugar, and let stand over night. In the morning pour off syrup and boil until quite thick; skim, then add tomatoes, ginger, and lemons which have been sliced and the seeds removed. Cook until tomatoes have a clarified appearance.

PICKLING.

Pickling is preserving in any salt or acid liquor.

Spiced Currants.

7 lbs. currants.	3 tablespoons cinnamon.
5 lbs. brown sugar.	3 tablespoons clove.

1 pint vinegar.

Pick over currants, wash, drain, and remove stems. Put in a preserving kettle, add sugar, vinegar, and spices tied in a piece of muslin. Heat to boiling point, and cook slowly one and one-half hours.

Sweet Pickled Pears.

Follow recipe for Sweet Pickled Peaches, using pears in place of peaches.

Sweet Pickled Peaches.

½ peck peaches.   1 pint vinegar.
2 lbs. brown sugar.   1 oz. stick cinnamon.
Cloves.

Boil sugar, vinegar, and cinnamon twenty minutes. Dip peaches quickly in hot water, then rub off the fur with a towel. Stick each peach with four cloves. Put into syrup, and cook until soft, using one-half peaches at a time.

Chili Sauce.

12 medium-sized ripe tomatoes.   1 tablespoon salt.
1 pepper finely chopped.   2 teaspoons clove.
1 onion finely chopped.   2 teaspoons cinnamon.
2 cups vinegar.   2 teaspoons allspice.
3 tablespoons sugar.   2 teaspoons grated nutmeg.

Peel tomatoes and slice. Put in a preserving kettle with remaining ingredients. Heat gradually to boiling point, and cook slowly two and one-half hours.

Ripe Tomato Pickle.

3 pints tomatoes peeled
   and chopped.   4 tablespoons salt.
1 cup chopped celery.   6 tablespoons sugar.
4 tablespoons chopped red   6 tablespoons mustard seed.
   pepper.   ½ teaspoon clove.
4 tablespoons chopped onion.   ½ teaspoon cinnamon.
                     1 teaspoon grated nutmeg.
2 cups vinegar.

Mix ingredients in order given. Put in a stone jar and cover. This uncooked mixture must stand a week before using, but may be kept a year.

Ripe Cucumber Pickle.

Cut cucumbers in halves lengthwise. Cover with alum water, allowing two teaspoons powdered alum to each quart of water. Heat gradually to boiling point, then let stand on back of range two hours. Remove from alum water and chill in ice water. Make a syrup by boiling five minutes two pounds sugar, one pint vinegar, with two tablespoons each of whole cloves and stick cinnamon tied in a piece of muslin. Add cucumbers and cook ten minutes. Remove cucumbers to a stone jar and pour over the syrup. Scald syrup three successive mornings, and return to fruit.

Unripe Cucumber Pickles (Gherkins).

Wipe four quarts small unripe cucumbers. Put in a stone jar and add one cup salt dissolved in two quarts boiling water and let stand three days. Drain cucumbers from brine, bring brine to boiling point, pour over cucumbers, and again let stand three days; repeat. Drain, wipe cucumbers, and pour over one gallon boiling water in which one tablespoon alum has been dissolved. Let stand six hours, then drain from alum water. Cook cucumbers ten minutes, a few at a time, in one-fourth the following mixture heated to the boiling point and boiled ten minutes : —

1 gallon vinegar.	2 sticks cinnamon.
4 red peppers.	2 tablespoons allspice berries.
2 tablespoons cloves.	

Strain remaining liquor over pickles which have been put in a stone jar.

Chopped Pickles.

4 quarts chopped green tomatoes.	3 teaspoons allspice.
¾ cup salt.	3 teaspoons cloves.
2 teaspoons pepper.	½ cup white mustard seed.
3 teaspoons mustard.	4 green peppers sliced.
3 teaspoons cinnamon.	2 chopped onions.
2 quarts vinegar.	

Add salt to tomatoes, let stand twenty-four hours, and drain. Add spices to vinegar, and heat to boiling point; then add tomatoes, peppers, and onions, and cook fifteen minutes after boiling point is reached.

Spanish Pickles.

1 peck green tomatoes
  thinly sliced.
4 onions thinly sliced.
1 cup salt.
½ oz. cloves.
½ oz. allspice berries.

½ oz. peppercorns.
½ cup brown mustard seed.
1 lb. brown sugar.
4 green peppers finely
  chopped.
Cider vinegar.

Sprinkle alternate layers of tomatoes and onions with salt, and let stand over night. In the morning drain, and put in a preserving kettle, adding remaining ingredients, using enough vinegar to cover all. Heat gradually to boiling point and boil one-half hour.

Chow-Chow.

2 quarts small green tomatoes.
12 small cucumbers.
3 red peppers.
1 cauliflower.
2 bunches celery.
1 pint small onions.
2 quarts string beans.

¼ lb. mustard seed.
2 oz. turmeric.
½ oz. allspice.
½ oz. pepper.
½ oz. clove.
Salt.
1 gallon vinegar.

Prepare vegetables and cut in small pieces; cover with salt, let stand twenty-four hours, and drain. Heat vinegar and spices to boiling point, add vegetables, and cook until soft.

Pickled Onions.

Peel small white onions, cover with brine, allowing one and one-half cups salt to two quarts boiling water, and let stand two days; drain, and cover with more brine; let stand two days, and again drain. Make more brine and heat to boiling point, put in onions and boil three minutes. Put in jars, interspersing with bits of mace, white peppercorns, cloves, bits of bay leaf, and slices of red pepper. Fill jars to overflow with vinegar scalded with sugar, allowing one cup sugar to one gallon vinegar. Cork while hot.